T0285221

"In a country thirsty for leadership, *Prepare for Impact* delivers! Chad and Ryan's insatiable passion for leadership will have you wanting to run out of the tunnel! Bravo!"

Frank Pacetta, author, *Don't Fire Them, Fire Them Up*

"Chad and Ryan are the perfect combination to write a breakthrough book in such an important field. Ryan's content is outstanding and is often cited by our sales team. Chad is simply the most impressive sales and business leader that I've encountered in professional sports. He's been a mentor to me and so many other folks in the industry. The Estis brothers focus on being authentic and high-integrity leaders in *Prepare for Impact*. In a world where most sales books are about tactics to hit near-term goals, this focus is so dearly needed. A must-read for the next generation of leaders."

Russ D'Souza, co-founder, SeatGeek

"Ryan and Chad's humility and heart-centered approach to leadership encourages us to reconsider previous sales and leadership paradigms. *Prepare for Impact* is grounded in actual life lessons and translates as clear, approachable, and easy to understand while still being thought-provoking and honest about the future. Ryan has been a sage advisor to my companies and a thought leader to our constituents. He's unarguably one of the best futurists and experts in the marketplace and this book is a must-read!"

Julie Faupel, founder and CEO, REALM

"I have had the privilege to witness the execution of the 30 Steps and 9 Tactics outlined in this book from a front-row seat. The beauty lies within the simplicity, which has resulted in the transformation of countless careers, franchises around the globe, and growth of the entire business of sports. Following the lessons within will lead to a lifetime of success, and, more importantly, help develop meaningful relationships, which is the true driver of joy."

Mike Ondrejko, President of Global Sales, Legends

"Being in the unique position of having a front-row seat for the Estis brothers' college years and early-career exploits, I can say their experience is not uncommon. Having shared their experience of navigating the transition from college to the corporate world and now meeting with upcoming graduates, I can say the fear of the unknown and lack of a clear playbook continues today. The beauty of *Prepare for Impact* is that it offers meaningful insight for a student preparing to transition, a young professional navigating their first stages of their career, and a thirty-plus-year veteran like me who needs to attract, develop, and mentor the teams of the future for our organization. Beyond the great utility of the book, it is also a great American story. It is truly a must-read!

Sam Chamberlain, Chief Operating Officer, FIVE GUYS

"In typical fashion, Ryan Estis absolutely knocks this one out of the park. In a world so often focused on shortcuts and short-term success, *Prepare For Impact* offers a playbook and potent reminder about what is required to build meaningful, sustainable relationships and sales growth for the long term. Ryan and Chad offer a dynamic, inspiring narrative with ideas you can implement immediately and that will ensure you are well positioned to thrive amidst change, challenge, and uncertainty in both business and in life!"

Karen Robertson, EVP, Fidelity National Financial

"Chad and Ryan are two of the most impressive people and professionals you will encounter. They have the EQ and IQ to adapt to changing business and leadership conditions in the moment and have bundled the 'answers to *that* test' in this book for us. I've been fortunate to watch them live the lessons of *Prepare for Impact* and be a benefactor of their tutelage along the way."

Eric Sudol, SVP Corporate Partnership, Dallas Cowboys and President/ CEO ProStar Energy Solutions

"Chad and Ryan are two of the most successful and humble business executives in the world. They have both risen from the bottom to the highest levels in their respective fields through decades of near flawless execution. Now we know how! *Prepare for Impact* unveils their completely fresh and innovative ideas and secrets in a story-led 'how-to' guide for CEOs, leaders, executives, and salespeople. The captivating tales will inspire you to lead with more compassion and purpose, while the tools and techniques will allow you to apply them in everyday life. It is nice to finally read a book that shows vulnerability and adversity can help you prevail."

Rob Wechsler, founder and managing director, Blue Star Innovation Partners

"In the new era of business, human-centered leadership is the only way to thrive in the face of turbulence and disruption. *Prepare for Impact* is the perfect book at the perfect time, helping us lead more effectively and with more meaning, driving both sustainable success and lasting impact. Ryan and Chad Estis strike a nerve, providing the ideal antidote to uncertainty and rapid change. Truly a masterpiece of modern leadership, for both business and life."

Josh Linkner, *New York Times* bestselling author, venture capital investor, five-time tech entrepreneur

"What sets *Prepare for Impact* apart is not only the knowledge and wisdom it imparts but also the inspiring journey of the Estis brothers themselves. Ryan and Chad exemplify the power of determination, commitment, and sibling rivalry turned collaboration. Their story resonates and serves as a testament to what can be achieved through hard work and a genuine passion for success. I highly recommend this book to anyone looking to enhance their sales skills, elevate their leadership capabilities, or simply seek inspiration to make a meaningful impact in their careers. It is a valuable resource that deserves a prominent place on every professional's bookshelf."

Ronda Conger, author, speaker, and Vice President of CBH Homes

"An entertaining read full of practical sales and leadership insight that can help you win. More importantly, Ryan and Chad offer perspective on what matters most—family, friendship, relationships, and enjoying the journey with people you respect and love."

Jesse Itzler, entrepreneur, author of *Living With a SEAL*

"Chad exemplifies the term *leader*, while simultaneously showing those around him what we should all aspire to be in our careers and in life. We have been training sales reps on the 30 Steps to Sales Success for the twenty-three years we have worked together. The 30 Steps and 9 Tactics for leadership are a playbook for everyone aspiring to climb the career ladder."

Doug Dawson, Senior Vice President of Sales and Service, Dallas Cowboys

"Ryan Estis has been a valued partner with our sales team at AmeriSource-Bergen. In *Prepare for Impact*, the Estis brothers share so much of what it takes to drive growth and impact customers in today's ever-changing marketplace. An entertaining read full of practical sales and leadership insight that I highly recommend for anyone looking to level up and create more impact!"

Rusty Massey, SVP, Specialty GPO Sales and Physician Services, AmeriSourceBergen

"*Prepare for Impact* is an entertaining take on practical habits we can all adopt to become a servant leader. Told through the success on their own journeys, the Estis brothers have created a guide for what we all strive to accomplish: living a life of purpose based off the impact we make on others."

Delanie Foley, Senior Director of Events, AT&T Stadium

"Whenever I find myself in need of guidance and a fresh perspective to navigate my business through transformative times, one voice consistently stands out: Ryan Estis. For the past fifteen years, I have personally witnessed the practicality and effectiveness of the ideas and strategies presented in this book. These insights are not mere theories conceived in a controlled environment; they have been forged in the real-world trenches of sales and leadership. In a world longing for a human-centered, heart-led approach, the Estis brothers have drafted the blueprint for the next generation of great leaders to follow. There's no denying that this book has arrived precisely when it is needed most."

Seth Mattison, founder, FutureSight Labs; co-founder, ImpactEleven

"*Prepare for Impact* is a powerful blend of sports smarts and leadership lessons, straight from the trenches. Chad and Ryan's focus on teamwork and results has shaped our work at SeatGeek, where Chad has been an invaluable mentor and advisor. This book is an honest, clear-cut guide for anyone looking to win and—just as importantly—win the right way."

Jack Groetzinger, co-founder and CEO, SeatGeek

"As an old friend, I've watched Chad and Ryan's extraordinary careers unfold with deep respect and awe, and I've witnessed their tremendous talent and success firsthand. But with *Prepare for Impact*, they've truly outdone themselves. This is not just a book; it's a toolkit for success. Chad and Ryan don't simply tell you how to achieve, they show you—with steps and tactics that can catalyze transformative results for any business. Their commitment to creating maximum impact and their passion for genuine, human-centered leadership shines through every page. Prepare to be impacted. This isn't just a must-read—it's a 'must-act.'"

Lance Tyson, #1 *Wall Street Journal* and *USA Today* bestselling author of *The Human Sales Factor*, President and CEO of Tyson Group

"I have known Ryan and Chad Estis for my entire professional career and lived the 30 Steps and 9 Tactics in action, real time. *Prepare for Impact* is not only a playbook on how to accelerate your sales or leadership career, but it is an honest story of the struggle, success, and profound growth that both Ryan and Chad have experienced along the way. It is tactical, thought provoking, and exactly what every top performer and leader should be reading. What a gift for all of us to learn from their journey!"

Lynn Mandinec, business manager for Ryan Estis

"In this book, the Estis brothers provide a strategic roadmap that should be required reading for business leaders at every level. The truth is that drive, commitment, tactics, and aggressiveness simply aren't enough. The common denominator for true success and fulfillment in the global business world today can only be found in winning cultures built on a foundation of ethics, teamwork, and true servant leadership. Sadly, this simple but crucial formula has been lost in much of business today, and the Estis brothers serve as a rare and strong beacon example to follow. They are leaders with a strong vision—and strong values—and this important book lights the way for future generations."

Jim Wilkinson, executive chairman, TrailRunner International

"As a leader, I found Chad and Ryan Estis's book to be both enlightening and inspiring. Their deep understanding of sales dynamics and leadership principles shines through every chapter. Reading this book is a transformative experience that will leave you equipped to tackle any business challenge with confidence."

Michael Yormark, President of Roc Nation Sports International

"Traditional models for growth and leadership are no longer effective in our forever-changed world. *Prepare for Impact* offers a practical, relevant, and human-centered approach for leading teams and driving growth into the future—which is precisely what is required today. Ryan and Chad offer a powerful path forward, forged in personal experience that will undoubtedly make the world of work a better place."

Peter Sheahan, C-suite adviser, keynote speaker, and VC partner

www.amplifypublishinggroup.com

Prepare for Impact: Driving Growth and Serving Others through the Principles of Human-Centered Leadership

Second printing. This Amplify Publishing edition printed in 2024.

For more information, please contact:
Amplify Publishing, an imprint of Amplify Publishing Group
620 Herndon Parkway, Suite 220
Herndon, VA 20170
info@amplifypublishing.com

Library of Congress Control Number: 2023912619

CPSIA Code: PRV0924B

ISBN-13: 978-1-63755-648-1

Printed in the United States

To our favorite teacher, Phyllis Estis, with love.
Mom, thank you for everything.

PREPARE FOR IMPACT

Driving Growth and Serving
Others through the Principles
of Human-Centered Leadership

RYAN ESTIS & CHAD ESTIS

WITH JIM EBER

an imprint of Amplify Publishing Group

CONTENTS

PART I: THE 30 STEPS

PART II: THE 9 TACTICS

PART I

THE 30 STEPS

CHAPTER 1

THE WRITING
ON THE WALL

Dude look at the wall

That's all Chad's text said. Then Ryan noticed the picture: "30 Steps to Success" painted on the wall of the offices of the Atlanta Falcons of the National Football League.

It had been twenty years since Ryan first typed up the original version of those steps for Chad after he told Ryan he was struggling in his first sales job. Now they were on the wall of a sports franchise worth billions.

What?! I can't even . . . Ryan thought. *WHY?* He texted back.

Why indeed. Look at Ryan's steps:

1.	Effort	17.	Know Your Competition
2.	Preparation		
3.	Education	18.	Know Your Clients
4.	Training	19.	Assume the Sale
5.	Practice	20.	Sell Yourself
6.	Presentation	21.	Enthusiasm
7.	Knowledge	22.	Relationships
8.	Questions	23.	Goals
9.	Sell the Benefits	24.	Teamwork
10.	Time Management	25.	Difficult Prospects
11.	Ask for the Order	26.	Mentoring
12.	Sell Past the No	27.	Surround Yourself with Successful People
13.	Deadlines		
14.	Follow-Up	28.	Don't Break Promises
15.	Correspondence	29.	One Final Call
16.	Customer Service	30.	Exercise

Aren't these steps kinda basic? Isn't the order they're in kind of random? Don't they say what other books already say? In the age of AI, big data, and machine learning, aren't some of them dated?

Those were the questions that ran through Ryan's head as he texted with Chad, but that was nothing new. We've both asked all those questions and more about the 30 Steps over the years. Even though they were the foundation for our success as we started our careers—even though they have been seen and used by thousands of people, many of whom we have never met—we struggled to accept them as the foundation for this book. We only made our peace with them when we realized the answer to those questions we asked as we picked apart the 30 Steps over the years is, "Yes—and that doesn't matter."

Of course, those steps are simple. Sure, with AI, big data, and machine learning, we are all a lot more sophisticated in the way we leverage data and insight to make decisions, organize teams, and drive growth than when Ryan wrote them. To that end, the simplicity of the 30 Steps might even be contrarian, because they aren't obsessed with being sophisticated—or innovative. They are just what they say they are: a list of incredibly simple things people can do to succeed.

Nobody had prepared either of us for the impact our professional lives would have on us. When Chad reached out for help, Ryan responded by writing a list of "30 Steps to Successful Selling" he followed to turn his flailing career around. They were never intended to be anything more than an act of brotherly love. What made the steps so powerful for Chad beyond that act is what has made them so essential to him and others as a training tool: when you have something to prove, expectations are high and results are paramount to your success. They help you focus on what is important.

If we had any questions about the timelessness of these steps, we reminded ourselves that the 30 Steps on the Falcons' wall is identical in many ways to Ryan's original. Sure, someone tweaked them, and that's great! Ryan doesn't claim any copyright on his steps, and we're thrilled when people are not only inspired by the original list but make the steps their own. Heck, Ryan has also changed them over the years. In his presentations, he has renamed steps, moved them around, revised some of the language to make them shorter or clearer, and updated some verbiage. We didn't do that in this book. We wanted to show that even as markets move, technology evolves, and the world changes, the core principles remain just as powerful as when Ryan wrote them, which is why they remain the writing on the wall more than two decades later.

And we don't just mean the writing on the wall in sales, where we started our careers. Look at the writing on another wall—this time the wall of the Dallas Cowboys, the first sports team to be worth $9 billion.

Chad does work for the Cowboys but was not the one responsible for painting the 30 Steps on the wall in their offices. The person who did, like the person who painted the identical one on the Falcons' wall, did not call it "30 Steps to Successful Selling," just "30 Steps to Success." We like that. While the list was built for sales, and some steps are sales oriented, mastering them can lead to overall success for anyone, regardless of function.

Simply put, the 30 Steps are a framework for success—a framework that allows you to be authentically you as you achieve that success. They dictate a process to follow, but they don't dictate who you or your team must be while following that process. They only require you to be the best version of yourself while you execute them. You can't fake the story you write using these steps. In fact, the steps themselves are a story—not just our story but a human story that can be written by everyone who adopts them and makes the steps their own.

We have met and hired countless people who are struggling today just like we did when we started and need these steps and the stories that surround them. They need to learn and prepare to compete and win in an environment where the customer decides whether you pass or fail. People may come into jobs with information at their fingertips that we could only dream of having when we were starting out, but they're still stuck. Especially when it comes to selling, which is a big reason these steps remain relevant today to the more than ten million sales professionals in the United States and the companies and industries that depend on them.

The only question is if you are just getting started, starting over, or feeling stuck where you are: Are you willing to do the work these steps require? Chad was and more. The steps compelled him to take responsibility for his own success by being accountable to what kind of effort he was putting in to execute at the highest levels.

The question then becomes: Are you willing to do the work to lead others and empower them to do the work these steps require? Because what does every organization do with its best people when they become successful? *Promote them into management.*

When you separate yourself from the proverbial pack, leadership opportunities happen. But when our first leadership opportunities presented themselves, no one prepared us for that impact either. No one asked us, "What kind of leader do you want to be? How would you run your team? How does that sound to you?" Leadership training? Nope. It was like when we started our first jobs: Just *go.* Only this time, neither of us had a list to guide the other.

Organizations are filled with leaders both new and established who want to do a good job—to do right by their people and deliver big results. Most leaders genuinely want to build a team and culture in which people are excited to invest their time and talent and commit to something bigger than themselves. And yet, like us when we started, even though we had the 30 Steps to use as a foundation, they struggled. *Why?* Because the 30 Steps, or *any* steps, may prepare you for the road ahead, but they do not create a culture of success. Creating that culture requires a human-centered vision and leadership philosophy that supports things like the 30 Steps and the people executing them.

So, as we started writing this book, we asked ourselves: *What does it take to be an effective leader today? What are the essential skills and tactics that positively influence culture, fuel performance, and drive growth? What do people want from the work experience today, and how can we as leaders help them achieve their potential at work and fulfillment in life?* From those discussions, we created a new list, together, that became the second half of this book.

9 Tactics for Being a More Human-Centered Leader

1. Focus on Their Development
2. Go for Coffee
3. Practice Transparency
4. Create Safety
5. Build a Team Environment
6. Create Connection—Have Fun!
7. Be Vulnerable
8. Have Tough Conversations
9. Be Decisive

These nine tactics are the essential things we feel leaders need to do to create a culture that people can't wait to get up and get to work in—and keep them "all in" once they get there. We are talking about the kind of environment that has people wanting to contribute, stretch to reach their full potential, and deliver big results. Like the 30 Steps, they are neither comprehensive nor perfect, but they're ours, and we own them from both our work perspectives today.

Creating this list of tactics was neither quick nor easy for us, but that's what made the process so much fun: we did it together. We don't just have parallel career tracks—one of us making a living talking about sales and leadership, the other living it every day—we challenge each other to keep learning and growing. We are more than brothers. We are best friends. We travel together. Support each other in the most important moments, personally and professionally, no matter how busy we are or how many miles separate us. Ryan was the best man at Chad's wedding and was there when Chad brought his first child home from the hospital. Chad flew to be by Ryan's side when a health scare left him rattled. When Chad wondered what to do when he got an offer from the Jones family to join the Dallas Cowboys, Ryan dropped everything to talk him through making the decision. When Ryan left a fifteen-year career as an ad agency executive to launch his own business, Chad was on the phone with him until midnight talking things through. Chad even hired Ryan: after Chad took the Cowboys job and Ryan was established in his second career, Chad invited him to speak to the leadership team—more than once!

But before we were adults? *We hated each other.* Which is where our story and deeper dive into the 30 Steps begin.

CHAPTER 2

OH BROTHER(HOOD)

IT WAS 6:00 A.M. and still dark on a brisk Dallas morning when we came over the hill and saw the football field. We had established the workout the night before: sixteen wind sprints. Line up, sprint the field, walk the end zone, line up, go again. We approached the field with the unspoken understanding this wasn't just a workout; the race was on, as it always is with us. Growing up had been a daily exercise in competition. Our two-year age difference initially resulted in a big advantage for Ryan, like in his signature third-round knockout of Chad in the Thrilla in Aurora, Ohio (for the record, boxing gloves are a terrible Christmas gift for young boys). But Ryan never held back, and Chad never quit. Ryan says this made Chad tough, and he is. And when age no longer gave Ryan an edge, he paid the price for instilling that toughness in his brother.

"It didn't matter that I hadn't run a one-hundred-yard dash in a decade. I knew Chad wanted to run me into the ground, and I was determined that wasn't going to happen."

The first sprints felt good. By number five, we were both hurting. Hamstrings tight. Lungs burning. By number ten, Ryan realized he was going to vomit. He looked at Chad. Chad had to be feeling the same thing but looked all in. We lined up for sprint number eleven. Ryan knew there would have to be a medical emergency or death before one crossed the finish line and the other didn't: "You just realize at some point that you would rather die right there before you quit in front of your brother."

As intense as this race and all our competitions are as adults, they lack any of the jealousy and animosity common in a sibling rivalry. It wasn't always that way. We grew up close. Maybe not as close as our beds in the room we shared in our middle-class suburb of Cleveland, but still close—our lives united by a love for playing basketball and our inability to be good enough at anything we did in our father's eyes. Our dad was a health and physical education teacher for troubled kids. Our mom was a second-grade teacher, then a stay-at-home mom, and then a teacher again. Education was our household currency, and when Ryan decided to stop trading in that currency as a teenager, things got bad in our house. Ryan was angry and rebelled. He went out drinking. Came home past curfew. Boycotted homework, telling his teachers he'd be happy to take any tests but wouldn't give them time outside the classroom.

"*Loser.*" That was Chad's perception of Ryan at the time. "I couldn't wait for him to leave for college—assuming he even graduated high school. He was so far from what I wanted to be. He would come home, and I would say, 'What's wrong with you?' And he would say, 'What's wrong with *you*?' We didn't see eye to eye on anything. By the end of high school, we didn't even play basketball together."

To Chad's relief, Ryan did end up (barely) graduating and getting into Ohio University—and more importantly, he enrolled. He went because that was his parents' expectation, and he saw no other way to get out of the house, away from them and Chad. Ohio University was three and a half hours away—a nice, safe distance. But the taste of freedom only amplified Ryan's rebellion. He partied hard. He skipped class. He found himself on the verge of flunking out.

Meanwhile, Chad thrived at home. Ryan had been doing everything "wrong" in our father's eyes, so Chad did everything "right" to please him. As a result, when Ryan returned from college after his first year, things couldn't have been more tense. Chad was the "golden boy," and Ryan was the misfit who dropped the classes he was failing and didn't even complete a full freshman year.

Our parents told Ryan they were not going to pay for college if it continued: "You passed art history. You have no major. Turn it around or live at home and go to the community college." That was Ryan's wake-up call. No way he was staying home. He *liked* being at Ohio University, partying and playing basketball four nights a week. He just didn't really like the academic part. But knowing he needed to change didn't mean he knew how, and when Ryan returned for his sophomore year, he started to fall into the same bad habits. That's when one of the guys Ryan played basketball with invited him to come with him and check out a fraternity. Ryan ended up not only liking the frat but joining—and finding the support system he lacked. This fraternity partied but also had an expectation that you got decent grades and participated in activities around campus. Ryan did the work—in the classroom and on his attitude—and began to change his ways.

Not that Chad saw that change—or cared—until the university's siblings weekend the following spring. The fraternity did a big celebration around the weekend to show itself off and recruit future students. Ryan thought he should at least invite Chad, who was now a senior in high school, but Chad was hesitant. He had ruled out Ohio University, if only because he didn't want to go where Ryan went. But Chad decided the right thing to do was accept, and the weekend changed everything. We played basketball again. We hung out. We went to the fraternity party. Chad even liked Ryan's friends. Chad was so taken with it all he ended up going to Ohio University. He joined the fraternity when he started and was determined to make the school's NCAA Division I basketball team as a walk-on his sophomore year.

Our parents were so proud of Chad's determination, they gave him a free pass from working during the summer after freshman year so he could practice. That rekindled a bit of our rivalry. Ryan was doing double shifts in a restaurant to earn his spending money and would come home, crap from the kitchen all over his clothes, see Chad shooting hoops in the driveway, get totally pissed off, and scream some version of, "What are you doing? Don't waste your time out here. You'll never make it. You have no chance."

But Chad just smiled and proved he had the confidence, work ethic, and, of course, the desire to prove Ryan wrong whenever he had the chance. He made the team as a walk-on.

Road to Nowhere

While Chad enjoyed his first year at college, Ryan faced an uncertain future in his final one. As a sophomore, Ryan had seen the seniors in the frat going out on job interviews, preparing for the next phase of their lives. Junior year, he had a typically terrible sales internship in which he did and learned nothing about the business except how to be a gofer. Now a senior himself, Ryan had no idea where he was going or why. There seemed to be some secret for success that he didn't understand, and no one to tell him how to unlock it. "Our parents were of no help," Ryan says. "They were teachers. They believed in what they were doing, but they went to school every day of their lives.

They simply didn't have any business acumen or ability to guide us. They gave up so much for us and our sister, Brooke. They lived paycheck to paycheck. They took out a second mortgage and entered full-blown survival mode to pay for our college education. They were more worried about buying groceries next month than what we were going to be doing in a few years."

Chad remembers having the same feeling heading into college: "I swear to God that if you asked me when I was in college what I wanted to do, I would've said I want to be in business. If you asked me what kind or part of business, I had no clue, no capability of answering the question any further. I saw people in suits going into office buildings and thought, *I would like to have a briefcase and a suit on and go walk into one of those buildings every day.* But I had no idea what was going on inside. It was crazy how little we knew and how naive we were. We used to drive around Hudson, a wealthy town near ours that has all these big houses. We would've done anything to live like that. We had conversations about those houses hundreds of times. Could there be a way for us to have them?"

"Chad used to yell, 'There are one hundred houses right there. If those people can do it, then why shouldn't I be able to do it?'" Ryan laughs. "We used to talk about going door-to-door and asking them, 'What do you do? How did you get here?' Chad still wants to. Maybe the next book."

The fraternity helped Ryan a little, connecting him with people in business to learn about career opportunities. But nobody seemed to understand on any deep level why they made their career choices. Like so many college graduates, many of them just followed the choices of the brothers before them and the promise of money, which seemed a distant promise for Ryan—he graduated right into a recession. With little to go on, he looked at the nice houses and cars people in sales had and decided, *Okay, I'm going into sales. That's what I'm going to do.*

Ryan ended up getting an entry-level sales job in Minneapolis at a national advertising agency—$21,000 a year plus commission. On his first day, the company gave him a phone and a recipe box filled with leads. He listened to his boss do a pitch once and was sent on his way. Nine months into the job, he hadn't made a sale.

"It was a tough start. But it wasn't because I lacked desire. I got in early and stayed late. I did everything asked of me. I just had no clue and no support. My manager was telling me, 'I can't carry you for much longer.' I had eighteen dollars in my bank account. I didn't think I might fail. *I was failing.*"

That's when fate intervened: Ryan's buddy called him and said he had an extra ticket to see a motivational speaker at the convention center. *Who the hell wants to hear a motivational speaker?* he thought and almost passed. But there was a free happy hour, with food, so he was in. "I crushed three beers, ate a bunch of wings and cheese, and went into this room with about one thousand people, prepared to bail at the first break."

Then Jim Rohn took the stage, and Ryan sobered up quickly.

Wake-Up Call

Ryan felt an immediate connection to everything Jim Rohn was saying. Rohn had started his career in human resources for a big company and then as an entrepreneur before he became an author and one of the country's most sought-after speakers on professional development. Ryan had never been exposed to information like what Rohn presented. He grabbed a pen and started writing down everything Rohn said: success, goals, and planning. Commitment and sacrifice. Trust and relationships. Differentiating between effort and value. Ryan felt like Neo in *The Matrix*, learning career kung fu, shaking from the information being pumped into his brain.

At the end of his talk, Jim Rohn recommended two books: *Think and Grow Rich* and *The Richest Man in Babylon*. He told the audience of one thousand people that only two hundred of them would go out and read them in the next month, and that only fifty of those two hundred would take massive action based on their ideas and what they had heard tonight over the next year. "Those fifty people will be different from the other nine hundred fifty people in this room," Rohn said. Ryan was determined to be one of those fifty. Jim Rohn had given Ryan permission and guidance on how to be successful—and responsible for his own success—when no one else had.

Ryan bought Jim Rohn's books on tape that night and the two books he recommended the next day and became relentless about self-education and self-improvement. "I realized immediately that I would have an edge if I could learn and practice what I learned. Every time I got in the car it was books on tape, not music. I read every night before I went to bed. I made flash cards with sales objections on them and wrote down my best rebuttals as I went through them. I developed my own sales scripts. I practiced sales skills on anyone I could, even girls I dated, which was maybe not the best choice, but I was crazy about it. Obsessed. I had confidence I never had before. I set goals for the week, month, year, and five years ahead. Pretty soon I was no longer about to get fired; I was getting *paid*. Eighteen months later I was the number-one account executive in the company, and I knew I was never *not* going to be the number-one salesperson. I was going to break every record."

During the time Ryan moved up to an entirely different level at his company, Chad had graduated and started his first job working for the NBA's Cleveland Cavaliers. He had been close to becoming a basketball coach after graduation, but he ended up choosing sales. "I had an undergrad internship in sports administration with the Cavs and ended up taking an entry-level sales job there for a lot of the same reasons people take jobs: because my brother was in sales and people at school and in the sports industry said I should start in sales. I was living at home because they were paying me less than Ryan got when he started: sixteen thousand dollars a year and no benefits and almost no training. I was put at a desk with a script; given a list of numbers, a ruler, and a highlighter; and told to make one hundred cold calls a day. I got a half day to listen to other people do their calls, and then they said *go*."

Chad was still determined to succeed. When he had been this determined in the past, he had been successful. *This would work out too*, he told himself. That's what coming from our little town and walking on to become a two-year starter at a Division I basketball team had taught him: You just put your head down and do the work. That's how you get your reward. But Chad discovered that while hard work is useful, if you lack the skill for the task, it doesn't matter. You're just pounding your head against the wall. "Every day I went in with almost no success rate. I would get on the phone and feel sick. People weren't expecting my calls and didn't want to talk to me. I hated rejection. My confidence was gone. I was twenty-three years old and living at home and had no idea what I was doing."

Chad needed help. He knew Ryan had gone through something similar and turned it around. He called his brother.

"Ryan, what do I do?"

Stepping Up

As Chad and Ryan spoke, Chad sounded almost unrecognizable. He didn't just lack enthusiasm for what he was doing; he was intimidated, overwhelmed, and defeated. The tone in Chad's voice took him back to the days before he had heard Jim Rohn speak: Working hard but lacking the competency to succeed—close to being fired and back in our parent's basement, arguing with our father and selling baseball cards for beer money. He understood why Chad was stuck. No one at college had helped him connect what he learned to anything Jim Rohn or anyone else he was reading and listening to today was saying. Ryan also knew that more likely than not, no one at the Cavs could help Chad. They, like the people in Ryan's organization who achieved success, weren't aware of what they were doing to succeed and thus couldn't teach it. They didn't codify it into a system.

Ryan, what do I do?

"I got you. I know exactly what you need to do. We'll attack this."

That night, Ryan sat down and wrote a letter to Chad. "Here's what you need to do . . ." it began. What followed was a stream of consciousness about how sales drives business and the economy and gives people like them, sons of teachers from a town nobody knows in Ohio, the opportunity to make plenty of money and live a great life. He wanted Chad to love sales like he did—to be *grateful* he gets to do what he's doing. He told Chad that to become great takes more than just hard work; it requires a different mindset: "Sales is about confidence, and confidence starts on the inside, which is why state of mind when approaching a sale is as important as anything else."

Ryan then started boiling down everything he had experienced and learned into a list of steps for Chad to follow. The steps reflected Ryan's hunger for and immersion in learning about all kinds of business and positive thinking. They distilled all the stuff Ryan had highlighted and dog-eared in books and worn out the Walkman and the tape deck in his car listening to. They reflected the timeless tenets of thought leaders like Dale Carnegie, Napoleon Hill, Tony Robbins, Zig Ziglar, Og Mandino, and countless others. All the knowledge Ryan had filtered through his own experience, tailored to his needs, and used to break every sales record his company had.

Ryan had never codified anything he had done before. He was Jerry Maguire long before the movie, pacing in his apartment, vibrating with ideas. He paced and sat, paced and sat, pouring everything he had into refining them. When he was done, he called the list "30 Steps to Successful Selling."

Ryan mailed the letter and the 30 Steps the next day, hoping Chad would welcome them openly, get his mojo back, and kick ass. He did. He used them exactly as Ryan hoped: to understand the psychology of sales, overcome fear and resistance, shift his mindset, and play the "game" the right way.

"I read the 30 Steps from Ryan and immediately thought, *I need this to learn how to be a great salesperson*," Chad recalls. "The 30 Steps made me realize there was a skill set I needed to get better at and gave me the confidence that I *could* get better *if* I really put in the work on each one of them."

After lacking direction and facing the stress of failure, Chad used the 30 Steps to own his success and started to rise in his career just as Ryan had years before. Ryan figured now that Chad was on his way, the steps would be consigned to the archives of their brotherhood history. After all, they were never meant to see more than his brother's eyes. As you know, Ryan was wrong.

CHAPTER 3

THE 30 STEPS
TO SUCCESS

THINK BACK TO THE STORY that opened the second chapter of
this book: the morning we lined up for those sprints in Dallas and
Ryan realized he would rather die before he quit in front of Chad.
That realization reflected a shared understanding that comes from
a lifetime of head-to-head competition. For years, we did an annual
athletic competition cleverly called the Annual.

The Annual took place on a weekend during which we scheduled
three events: an eighteen-hole golf match, which Chad had a big advantage in; a three-to-five-mile race, which Ryan knew he had to win to have
a chance at winning it all; and a game of one-on-one basketball, which
Ryan begrudgingly admits Chad was also better at. With age no longer
an advantage, Ryan had to reach deep inside to find the same resolve
Chad had developed from years of being the underdog just to stay in
the competition. In fact, the only time Ryan ever won the Annual was
the one time he beat Chad in golf. Before that, Chad used to say, "How
does it feel knowing you'll never beat me in a round of golf ever?'"

"My greatest round of golf ever. Ninety-one to ninety. It was a great day. The battle of the burn," Ryan recalls.

"You are the least competent golfer, and you took me down that day," Chad says, shaking his head. "I'm still pissed. Can we tell the story of when I had to tell you to keep your bag on the cart when we were in DC because you were going to quit right in the middle of our round?"

"Why do you have to hijack the story that's going in the book?"

"Because it gets lost."

Like we said, we love to compete, and we finished the sprints that day. Who won? Not important. Okay, Chad won. But competition really wasn't the point—or the whole point. It is partly about being able to compete. The world of work is a very competitive place for winning new business, time, attention, interest, investment, resources, jobs, promotions, market share, and opportunity. So, while we push each other beyond our limits to compete and reach our full potential, that doesn't mean we can't celebrate the shit out of each other. Honor each other. Respect each other. Make the time to support each other in everything we do. Purpose is having an abundance mentality: there *is* enough of almost everything for everyone to succeed, which is why we believe in connecting, sharing, and having a generous spirit in everything we do.

Simply put, reading the explanations of the 30 Steps that follow and executing them to the best of your ability *will* help you compete—and not just in sales—though as we have said before, we are all in the business of sales—but at your highest potential. That's the key to these steps: maximizing your potential.

Remember what we said in the opening of this book: the 30 Steps may be simple, but they work. Ryan refers to them as simple process discipline—a catalyst for creating momentum, going over rejection rebuttals, challenging assumptions, studying your customer's business, scripting your own approach. People who open themselves up to the 30

Steps get that. That's why it became the writing on those walls. That's why when Chad gives keynotes today, the 30 Steps slide gets the most response. People with decades of experience in sales email him afterward and say things like, "The 30 Steps slide is so helpful because it focuses on what's most important." Which is exactly what happened to Chad.

Before Chad committed himself to the 30 Steps, he wasn't being outworked by anyone. He came in early and left late. His problem was his mindset. He hated how selling made him feel. Selling, like business in general, is about results, and like Ryan before him, Chad was failing to get them. He was lost, and his results were nowhere too. That made him question himself and lose confidence.

The 30 Steps forced Chad to confront *how* he was working. They gave him focus, a plan, a direction—a purpose. They calmed him down and forced him to ask himself questions he never had before: What was he willing to do to change? Read something? Practice? Dedicate time to his relationships? Send a handwritten note? Before the 30 Steps, he would look at the phone and have a negative physical reaction. After, he would look at the phone and think, *Let's go!*

"I realized successful people don't just kill for an organization; they know how to kill the right way," Chad recalls. "I didn't have to beat everybody to work and stay so late that I was on a first-name basis with the light switch. I needed to be familiar with how I spent my time when the lights were on. Everything didn't have to be about closing a sale. I started thinking about effort and dedication level. I started setting goals that focused on the steps like building relationships, asking effective questions, and selling myself. I measured my days not by the number of tickets I sold but by the number of good conversations I had. Five good conversations every day? That was twenty a week and eighty a month I could turn into legitimate leads. If I sold nothing in a day but talked to five people, I would go home feeling refreshed and happy."

What Chad did was focus on process over results, using methods correlated to the 30 Steps that were relevant to his industry and true to who he was to generate results that exceeded expectations. You can, too, if you're willing to make the investment. Your first ten years in business are a time to invest in your development and create some career momentum. There are things we were willing to do in our twenties and when we started over in our careers that we don't have to do today. We have the freedom to choose now because we made the investment early on to pour all of ourselves into the work these steps require.

PREPARE FOR IMPACT

The power of the 30 Steps is in their cumulative effect. You can skip around as you read them, but we think it helps to read them all—even if you are doing them well. Take the time to ask yourself the questions that appear at the end of each step, look at the callouts running through them, and then decide where there might be an opportunity to level up.

---

1. Effort

How you put in and direct your effort—and understand the commitment it requires—is the difference maker for everything we have discussed to this point and everything moving forward. Be hyperobsessed about mastering and committing yourself to these steps and investing in your career, not just getting results. If you limit it to just getting results for an organization, then you are limiting your career. Instead, use your commitment to communicate your desire to succeed to the people you want to work for. Think of it this way: Chad doesn't just want people who want to work for the Dallas Cowboys because they are a great team. That doesn't communicate anything more than a desire for status. Chad wants people who want to take his job—who are willing to ask themselves, *What am I willing to invest to grow and achieve my full potential?*

PREPARE FOR IMPACT:
EFFORT

- How important is this job to you?
- How are you willing to invest in today to get where you want to be tomorrow?
- How much time outside the "norm" are you willing to commit to your skills and craft?

---

2. Preparation

Don't just have the will to win—prepare to win! Most salespeople are not adequately prepared. They fail to put enough time into their preparation and thus fail to understand customer expectations. Those expectations have evolved dramatically since Ryan wrote these steps, requiring even more thought, discipline, and customization in the preparation cycle—and value still matters more than anything else for long-term relationships. Of course, expectations also depend on what you're selling, whether it is a transactional, strategic, or a consultative sale.

In Chad's business, a transactional sale is a single sale for a product like season tickets, as opposed to sponsorships, which are more strategic. Those sales are still very much about volume. That requires honing your approach through repetition and preparation. Reps are given

82% of B2B decision-makers believe sales reps are unprepared.[1]

prequalified and financially capable leads, and the more calls and appointments they have with those people, the better. But they still need preparation. They need to build networks, follow up on referrals, and have customer relations management tools to make that preparation faster. They need to be ready to conduct a needs analysis over the phone and build a case during the discussion, which might lead to a sale or a follow-up appointment. The goal is frequency and efficiency without sacrificing any of the other steps to generate as many sales a day as possible.

Those sales used to be the case in Ryan's business too. It was "make thirty-five decision-maker contacts and have four or five appointments a week." Ryan even remembers being in and around Indianapolis one week and having twenty-one sales meetings. He drove up Sunday night and banged out four, five, six meetings a day. And he was *celebrated* for it. Customers today are more sophisticated and demand a higher degree of preparation on the part of the seller for strategic and consultative impact—and far too many sellers are entering those conversations underprepared. Unprepared for customers who are overwhelmed, crunched for time, and expect you to consistently deliver more value.

"I would never do that now. I *could* never do that now," Ryan says. "Back in those days, I wasn't prepared to have strategic, well-thought-out conversations with twenty-five different businesses in five days. I didn't *need* to. I could go into someone's office and say, 'Tell me a little bit more about your business.' It was common to use a template presentation, go in, learn about somebody's business and what they were doing, what their needs were, present our services, and then attempt to earn a trial and/or do something for them. It could all be done in one or two meetings, maybe a third for larger opportunities. Today if I made that Indianapolis trip, I would expect to have a couple of meetings, and my preparation would start weeks before, especially if I'm being referred or they know who I am. I need to research them, know their points of view and identify challenges and opportunities, have a story to tell, and develop some great questions to engage them in a customized way. I have to be ready to answer the question, 'What do you know about my business, and how are you going to make it better, add value, solve a problem, or move us into the future?' Because the expectation for being prepared is so much higher."

When we were both starting out in sales, this would have been unheard of—and unnecessary. Today it is expected. Step back and consider your approach to the sales process. As Ryan says, "Prepare to win or prepare to discount!" Today's customers expect depth of research and customization, insight, guidance, and advice. In addition, more people are touching a buying decision than ever before, and each one of the people influencing the outcome may have a different agenda driving the decision—oftentimes in direct conflict with another member of the decision team. According to Gartner, an average of eleven people are involved in each business-to-business purchase, up significantly from years before.[2] More preparation is required to meet all those people where they are and help them make those decisions.

This approach goes back to what we said at the start of these steps: more isn't better; better is better. Being prepared for every touch point with a potential customer is served by mastering much of what you've learned so far: knowing your product, engaging with open-ended questions mapped to an outcome objective, and being ready to take in information based on those questions to adjust what you're presenting to meet the needs of the customer.

"We obsess over how we can continually upgrade our approach. And it starts before the ink on the contract is dry," Ryan adds. "I was doing a deal with Tiffany & Co. and mall traffic had been down, sales a little bit challenged. *How do I understand what they are trying to do and need to do better? They talk about the Tiffany experience when you buy a diamond. What does that mean?* So I rolled into a store with a photographer, told the salesperson I got engaged, and that I wanted to buy a diamond. I now understood how a Tiffany diamond becomes a Tiffany diamond. I also could have an intelligent conversation on how to deliver that more effectively, and I documented for them what I saw was missing."

PREPARE FOR IMPACT:
PREPARATION

- How much time do you spend preparing and customizing for each prospective outreach to deliver value?
- How can you elevate the conversation to focus on value the customer cares about?
- How can you deliver the customization and personalization your customers expect?
- How can you help customers solve big problems or accelerate opportunities?
- How can you give more than the competition?
- How can you make it easier for customers to buy?

3. Education

This step is what saved Ryan and allowed him to write the 30 Steps for Chad. Whenever he hit a plateau, it was because he had relaxed his commitment to learning. That remains true to this day. Taking in information like Ryan first did when he saw Jim Rohn—and then being willing to act on the ideas that information imparts—moves you from self-awareness to self-improvement.

Today we both understand our education is never over, and so must you. Exercise your mind and stay mentally fit—not just when it comes to training (see step 4) and keeping up with local, national, and global changes in business but also how you think about yourself and the world around you. Get the books, subscribe to the channels, listen to the podcasts, and learn from the best. Be willing to be uncomfortable and try to test what you learn. Be sure to engage those you disagree with, too, to avoid confirmation bias and understand the differences—and different opinions and approaches— of those around you.

How much time should you spend on all this? Ryan says at least five hours a week; Chad says at least twenty minutes a night. We're both right: The point isn't the amount of time but your dedication. Put the time in your calendar and commit to it.

> Learning agility is a top predictor of high potential, but just 15% of the global workforce are highly agile.[3]

PREPARE FOR IMPACT:
EDUCATION

- How are you learning and getting better every day?
- How many hours of scheduled "learning time" is in your calendar this week?
- What are the last three things you read, listened to, or attended to show your commitment to self-education—and what did you do or change after you finished them?

---

4. Training

Stay in the learning lane! Staying in the learning lane means being in a constant state of learning and adaptation in everything you do. You know you need to train when it comes to technology—everyone must train on new technology and methods of communication to keep up. So do the same thing when it comes to the big picture of *you*—your self-awareness and how you do things.

The training we relied on for the marketplace when the 30 Steps were written is not the same as today; however, the need is more important today than it has ever been with an ever-changing business landscape. The skills and knowledge you have today will not serve you the same way in ten, five, or even one year. Not even close. "When I started in sales and drove around the Twin Cities to appointments, I was constantly listening to books on tape—yes, actual cassettes," Ryan recalls. "As I got a little bit of success, I decided to buy my first nice car. A BMW. I was stoked. But this was when they were putting CD players in all the cars. As I got behind the wheel, I asked the salesperson where the cassette player was. He said he didn't have one. '*Whoa, whoa,*

whoa. I have thousands of dollars invested in books on tape. I won't buy the car. I don't care what it costs to get one. I have to have a cassette player.' He thought I was crazy. Who wanted a cassette

> **Continuous training gives 50% higher net sales per employee.**[4]

player? But drive time was two-plus hours of training time for me a day. I listened to them over and over again. I can hear those people speak even today, telling their stories. I wore out those cassettes long ago, but today, even as I do more elaborate things like weeklong retreats for immersive learning, I still listen as I travel. Now I do it all on Audible, but I will always stay in the learning lane."

You likely spend hours a week in your car, on a train or bus, on your bike, in an airport, and/or walking on your way to and from work. This is valuable training time. Use this time as training on the skills you need and want to improve—whatever medium that is—and to motivate you and get you in the right frame of mind when you get wherever you're going. Be obsessive about it. Disrupt yourself before the marketplace or competition does it for you.

PREPARE FOR IMPACT:
TRAINING

- How much time did you invest in your skills this week?
- How much are you willing to invest in your skills in the next twelve months?
- What are you willing to give up?

5. Practice

Training is where you learn skills. Practice is where you apply that learning to prepare to win. Practice is about testing what you've learned, trying out pitches and presentations, preparing for the bad and the good, and working on things over and over so you are ready to see and seize opportunities and overcome resistance and obstacles in "game time." Think of it this way: Professional athletes spend about 90 percent of their time training and practicing and 10 percent of their time in competition. Most business professionals do the exact opposite, if they practice at all.

Ryan credits making practice part of his routine a big reason he moved up in the advertising agency (and throughout his career). He rehearsed sales scripts and mapped out questions, creating question trees and anticipating responses. He needed Chad to understand why just doing some training and then spending all your time competing for sales or opportunities wasn't enough to level up. That's why one of the first questions he asked Chad when they discussed the 30 Steps was, "If you were on the other end of your presentation, would you buy?" Chad didn't know. He had never heard how he sounded to a customer. Ryan explained that was because Chad hadn't practiced, and he laid out a process to correct that.

"Ryan told me to stand in front of the mirror and do my opening pitch for season tickets and see how I sounded," Chad recalls. "He made me think about how I was handling every situation, answer, and objection, write it down, and study it. But his biggest thing and the most painful for me was hearing how you sound, because then you understand how the person on the receiving end heard you. He made me take everything I wrote down, record myself answering objections over things like price, and then listen to my responses. All this was foreign thinking to me. Practice what I was being asked to do at work all day? But then I remembered: practicing my shots in the driveway all afternoon was how I prepared to walk on to the Ohio basketball team. It is all about getting reps in before you need to use your skills to compete. I had done that as an athlete and knew the value of it, but I wasn't giving it the same value at work."

That lack of valuing practice is still pretty common in business today. If Ryan gathered everyone at most organizations he works with and asked how many of them made the effort to spend two hours practicing what they did that week, not many hands would go up. The reason is the same as it was for us back in the day: There is no connection between practice and results. Most people are taught that how you sell anything, including yourself, is about training, facts, and innate ability, when it is actually a skill that can be refined through practice. But the flow of any conversation is a learned skill, and if you never practice it—get those reps in—you'll never get better at it.

These reps shouldn't just be the responsibility of the account people. Leaders need to mandate that as a part of their business—and keep doing it themselves—which is something we talk about constantly and strive to do as leaders both to improve our teams and ourselves. We can bring in all the sales trainers we want to give our teams the tools to do the work, but if we don't mandate getting in some reps, too, it's not going to stick. For example, the Cowboys have an "accountability partner" program in which people are paired to help each other take responsibility for everything they do. When an entry-level salesperson comes in, part of their accountability partner's function is to role-play sales calls.

If you don't have a leader or company that mandates practice, do what Chad did and run practice drills and scrimmages with teammates or friends. Use their feedback to improve what you do. Practice your responses to their questions and objections, and then try your skills out in real life before you approach your customer.

- What percentage of your week is spent on practice each week?
- Where would you have been better served if you had practiced before you competed?
- Who is or can be your practice partner and holds you accountable?

6. Presentation

Early in his career, Chad was working a sales table at a press conference for a new player. It was a terrible place to be marketing. No one was showing up. The press wasn't buying anything. Hardly any fans came. He was just sitting there doing nothing when a guy from the organization who was three times his senior came up to him and asked how he was doing.

"Good," Chad said.

"Good?" the senior executive replied. "Well, see the skirt on this table? Do you think this looks good?"

Chad looked. The guy was right. It kinda looked like crap.

"When you are out here representing the organization, everything should be perfect. You should be representing us perfectly right now. Your material should be laid out perfectly, and the skirt on this table should be right."

Chad got it immediately. He was being disrespectful. He wasn't prepared.

The first impression and overall impression your presence makes come from more than your attire and grooming. They come from your body language, how you act toward others, and your attention to detail. You never know who is watching, regardless of whether the focus is on you or how much or how little is going on. The idea is to care deeply about the effort you put in and how you present that effort and the organization to others.

Chad has told everyone since, especially young people just starting out, that you may not think much about how you are creating a perception with others, but you are—always: "People who can and will have an impact on your future are watching. That shouldn't make you nervous, just aware. If you are paying attention to the 30 Steps and executing them, you will be making a good impression, and someday someone will tap you on the shoulder and say, 'How about this new opportunity?'"

Simply put, always remember how you show up to anything should be intentional. Pay attention to how your presence makes others feel.

In presenting to clients of all sizes, in person and virtually, Ryan has learned that respect extends to your energy. He can do one hundred events a year, but whether it is his tenth or hundredth presentation, it will always be his client's and audience's first. Every person you touch must feel like you are there just for them. Your probability is much lower, even with a great prospect, if your energy is off.

"I better be 'that guy' when I walk out onstage," Ryan says. "I have to be conscious of the physical, mental, and emotional energy people get from my presence. I have to show up as the best version of myself every time. When you decide to show up consistently as the best version of who you are, it gives you your best opportunity to meet people where they are."

PREPARE FOR IMPACT:
PRESENTATION

- What's the first impression you make?
- How did you show up?
- How is your presence affecting others?

7. Knowledge

This step is not about knowledge in terms of facts. Yes, you must know everything you are doing and selling by heart. But product information is accessible to anyone today. Why do clients and customers need you if all you are going to do is recite information, benefits, and amenities that anyone can get from a website? You bring no value that way. Customers want insight. They want guidance. People are afraid to make a mistake when they buy. The best salespeople are teachers with the ability to synthesize complex information and convey it in a way that elevates the customer's confidence in making a buying decision. Your job is to connect their needs to solutions that your product—or service, or organization, or *you*—can provide. That's what the best sellers do: Leverage their expertise. Challenge and say, "Here's why it will be better for you." Anticipate questions a prospect might ask and what the best answers and examples are to demonstrate value. To do this, you must be the expert in

43% of buyers say it's an immediate deal killer if sellers don't understand their own products and services.[5]

others' needs, not just what you're pitching. How you discover their needs also requires the steps that follow, including asking effective questions and having a deep understanding of the customer and marketplace. Remember: our job, at its core, is to help people make the right decision.

"For me, it's always about how far a sales rep can go without any assistance," says Chad. "Can you give the benefits and amenities and get an appointment? Good but not enough if you don't have the knowledge to close the sale. Go make the sale? Great. But what are you doing to close that sale? How are you always looking to execute product and organizational knowledge at a higher level? When someone asks you about a deal and has a series of contract or legal questions, do you attack those questions and take the deal over the finish line, or do you succumb to fear, doubt what you know, and turn them over to someone else? Attacking is about effort and confidence when it comes to product knowledge."

PREPARE FOR IMPACT:
KNOWLEDGE

- What do you know that your customers don't that will compel them to think differently about their own future and opportunities for success?
- How can you get closer to them?
- How have you prepared to help the customer make the very best decision?

8. Questions

Effective questions are open-ended questions, which are the key to sales and developing relationships in general. Questions that open people up are more effective than yes-no questions. *Ask* those open-ended questions and then *listen* to the answers. You will keep people engaged longer, generate more interest and enthusiasm in you and what you're selling, and develop a stronger connection if you ask effective questions to get to know people and understand their thoughts, needs, fears, goals, dreams, and resistance. That will provide you with the information you need to earn the right to make the best recommendation.

This is precisely why Chad trains and drills his teams on having conversations that never ask yes-no questions, because when you develop skill with questions accompanied by active listening you really can positively impact all your relationships. It all starts with who, how, what, and why. Then learn to follow up, prompt, and probe. A "tell me a little more about that" keeps a conversation going every time.

"Really good salespeople are listening to the answers and picking up on all the keys they're going to use to unlock resistance and close the sale," says Chad. "All it takes is a few pieces of information from a few effective questions to match them with what they are trying to sell, which is why I started learning how to talk to administrators to get information about the companies and their decision-makers. If I couldn't get a name, I would at least find out if they had tickets to the other professional teams in town, and if the answer to that was *yes*, then they would move up on my lead list. It was tactical but it was smart, and it started with asking questions the right way."

There are lots of books that cover having skill with questions, building out question trees, and creating question architecture on a deeper level than this step. To get started here, you need to know a great question is not one that everyone asks but one that connects to the person you are asking. Instead of asking someone you meet, "What do you do?" ask, "What do you like to do when you're not working?" That connects you to what they are most passionate about and gives you an opportunity to connect to that person at a place of highest need and probe for more: Why do you feel that way? What gives rise to that? The same questions can be used in sales to sell from a position of intelligence. The more you know, the better prepared you are to be effective at the next steps.

PREPARE FOR IMPACT:

QUESTIONS

- Can you get through an entire day or even a week without asking one yes-no question?
- How can you turn a yes-no question you ask into something that starts a conversation and shows interest in the person you're talking to?
- What are your very best questions?

9. Sell the Benefits

This step is all about one word: *value*. Sell value, not price; explain the features, but sell the benefits. Customers don't buy on price; they default to price in the absence of value and a quality experience. You must give people compelling reasons and evidence to buy into your ideas. We are all naturally resistant to change. But we will usually decide to buy or make that change based on a few elements or criteria that connect to our needs or problems. Will it save time? Money? Earn them a promotion? You must identify those needs and problems

After a presentation, 63% of attendees remember stories. Only 5% remember statistics.[6]

and create a vision of the desired or improved future state connected to your product or solution.

When selling something experiential, the buying and selling process should also be an experience. Chad first learned this while working his way up in the Cavaliers organization. He was selling luxury suites, but the Cavs weren't great, and the market for suite buyers was worse. Chad then reconsidered how the team had been selling those suites: Calling potential customers, trying to get into their offices for meetings, visiting them with pamphlets and brochures to show the perks and amenities of the suite, and then seeing if they'd buy. The success rate of those meetings was low and lacked any connection to the experience of being at the game. So Chad and his team flipped the script start to finish and changed the dynamic before the discussion even started. They invited potential customers to come to the Cavs offices at the arena. Chad wanted to see themselves as part of the Cavs. They sent cars that pulled into where the players parked and escorted customers past their potential suites, focusing their interest on what the Cavs had to offer and understanding their interest and what they wanted. That led to much better discussions before the formal presentation began. The closing rate was so much higher. Chad adapted this approach for every team he has worked with since, working closely on each detail of the experience so they saw the benefits to them.

"What Chad did was tell them a story, not just sell them on one," Ryan says. "Storytelling is a critical competency to achieving sales mastery. If you are selling season tickets, you need to get out of the business of sight lines and sections and other low-hanging BS and make the guy imagine being in the seats when the Cowboys score the touchdown that sends them to the Super Bowl again. And when it happens, you want that guy to think what it would be like if he was hugging his boy at the game the minute it happened. And telling his boy the story that his old man took him to the game when Troy Aikman took them to the Super Bowl. Storytelling creates that connection with emotional resonance."

PREPARE FOR IMPACT:
SELL THE BENEFITS

- What is the benefit to the customer of using you or what you are selling?
- How can you convey that in an experience or story that makes what you're selling memorable? Can you prove it with a case study or client example?

10. Time Management

When Ryan started his own business, he had grown tired of sitting at his kitchen table feeling isolated. So he started going to a nearby Starbucks every day to work and connect with others. One day Ryan was leaving that Starbucks when Chad called—and called him out.

"Dude, if you could figure out a way to get paid from having networking and brainstorming meetings at Starbucks all the time, you'd be crazy rich."

The truth hurt.

It was only after Chad called Ryan out that he realized how he had rationalized spending so much time having those loosely defined

82% of people
don't use any
time manage-
ment system.[7]

networking meetings: *Two hours burned talking with a blogger? We traded ideas. It felt good. Hey, I was out of the house, making connections and meeting people.*

"I realized I had to take back control of time," Ryan says. "I was becoming a professional coffee shopper.

"Coffee shopping meant avoiding the hard, isolating work at the kitchen table that was required of a new entrepreneur. Sure, meeting new people, learning about their work, and figuring out if we can support each other is important to my business. Most of my business comes from referrals, so having an open approach to networking makes sense for me. But it's easy to substitute 'networking' or any other 'business-related' work for the real hard work that fires up the growth engine inside the business."

Are you coffee shopping? Time management is about performing *and* prioritizing—protecting your calendar and putting more structure and better systems in place. An absence of routine leads to chaos.

The best way to start managing your time is at the beginning. Whether it is exercising, meditating, journaling, reading, spending time with your kids, or organizing your day, if your morning routine is intentional—and positive—it will put you in the right mindset. When Ryan wrote these steps, his morning routine, though he never called it that, was about getting up early, getting in some thought-provoking and stimulating content, and then being the first one into the office. Get an advantage—win the morning, win the day. Chad took that to heart, which is why he called Ryan out when he fell into coffee shopping.

Today our routines may be more about preparation, relationships, and taking care of ourselves than getting in early, but they are just as intentional—and necessary. To avoid falling into the coffee-shopping trap in 2020, when working from home became a thing of the present for many of us, Ryan and his business manager, Lynn, scheduled a half day each week where they only did outside sales activity. Everything else got shut down. No responding to emails or texts, no taking phone calls. That structure quadrupled their results by focusing them and making their most important activity a priority.

If you find your calendar consumed with your version of coffee shopping, audit it and ask where you can be more productive. But don't eliminate the benefits of intentional meetings to do quality networking, having important conversations outside the office, or just taking a break. A good day plan also includes "white space." Instead of scheduling back-to-back sales calls and meetings, give yourself a little time during the day to think strategically and respond to any true crises that may come up. Take short breaks to walk around, go outside, or get a glass of water. Work in fifty-minute bursts. That will leave you refreshed and ready to tackle the next challenges throughout the day.

Simply put, you must make everything you put effort into *intentional*—relationships, celebrating wins, training, practicing, making that pitch, even relaxing and vacation. You need to focus on all your daily routines and rituals to make them more intentional, which is why this step appears here and not earlier or later. To put effort into the steps we have covered so far, you must schedule time for them. That's mission critical to maximizing opportunities for success. Every activity should be about improving the chance for and getting to your desired outcome. Waste too much time on compliance items like data entry and expense reports, and you lose opportunities. Spinning your wheels too long on low-yield or no-yield activities, doing only what feels comfortable, keeping leads in a warm position, and not getting to a decision to close a sale or move, and you jeopardize your performance.

TIME MANAGEMENT

- How intentional is your daily routine?
- Are you prioritizing your day parts with the most important work?
- Do you have white space to think, create, and reset?

11. Ask for the Order

Chad has watched salespeople do the other twenty-nine steps and then not ask for the order, because of one word: *fear*. They hold their leads in a "warm position" so they don't go home at night facing rejection. That makes them feel better about themselves. But they don't go home celebrating success either. Chad never understood this. "I hated the unknown," he says. "I wanted to make people say yes or no today to free me from the unknown. Then I could move to the next step and sell past the no and get the order, or I could move on. You don't need to do a needs and benefits analysis to ask for the order. It's appropriate to ask for the order at any given time. Understand that all you are having is a genuine conversation."

Ryan couldn't agree more. "That conversation is how you ascertain that you are the right fit for what the client wants. Sometimes you aren't the right choice, and that's okay. Clarity breeds confidence, and ambiguity is the kiss of death. Warm leads just keep burning cycles of time. Mediocre salespeople are comfortable in that ambiguity."

> 90% of customers won't buy unless you ask.[8]

That said, plenty of talented salespeople end up missing their quotas because they hesitate to ask for or do anything that might make someone and/or themselves uncomfortable. Warm is safe, and our brains are wired for safety and comfort. This is why so many deals go to die in the land of indecision.

Have a stalled lead? Make a commitment to move them into a yes or a no as soon as possible and close every qualified opportunity. Give someone the chance to say yes or no. Have a go-to question that moves people to a yes or no decision (if no, see the next step). You're doing this to earn a commitment, not to share information. Fight past the fear of rejection and say something like, "Obviously, we are meeting today because I want your business. If I were able to demonstrate value and that we were a better solution at your price point, can you see any reason we wouldn't move forward with an agreement today?" If they say that's a lot, ask them to tell you about that. You must be willing to engage that resistance and get uncomfortable—to enjoy those moments of tension and silence when you are waiting for someone to answer and get to a yes or no.

PREPARE FOR IMPACT:
ASK FOR THE ORDER

- How can you overcome any fear of rejection and ask for the order?
- How can you move your prospects out of the "warm position" and into a yes or a no?

12. Sell Past the No

Studies show most sales are closed after overcoming multiple signs of resistance. Yet most sellers give up after the first or second sign of resistance because it's uncomfortable. Fail to get a piece of business or lose a pitch, and they shut it down. But a no in sales is often just the first sign of resistance and a request for additional information. You need to uncover what the resistance is and eliminate it through effective questions and selling the benefits of what you offer. When you do, you begin to consider the word *no* a sign of interest and a request for additional information—and even push back a little with the customer to get them to a decision. In fact, you almost welcome tension, and it actually gets fun!

It helps to consider the psychology of selling. You learn to play a game with *yourself* to keep you focused on the task and break it down like Chad did when he started measuring success by conversations, not results: *If I make one hundred dials, I'm going to get ten people on the phone and get three to five appointments with great conversations. Go.* That's a framework that gets you comfortable and builds up resistance to rejection. It also informs how many conversations you need to have to hit your target. You can learn to frame each call as a challenge as you move prospects past their initial resistance and get those appointments. This works even when person-to-person networking, getting referred from relationships, or getting found through your marketing.

"When Ryan helped me understand sales is a game like sports that I needed to play better, I realized I could even be a little bit challenging," says Chad. "When someone said something I didn't want to hear, I didn't have to apologize, say, 'Have a good day,' and hang up. I could hang in there past the no and try to make something happen that I believed would benefit the customer."

We cannot emphasize that last line enough: The age of getting someone to buy or do something that may not be in their own best interest is over—or should be. When Ryan wanted Chad to see sales as a game, it was about competition, not deception, which has no place in a quality sales organization. In the past, we heard bosses flat-out tell salespeople to exclude important points, tell partial truths, and even lie just to get that one sale. Wrong move.

Selling is not about manipulation. Back when we created the steps, a lot of sales trainers taught closing techniques like the puppy dog close, the Ben Franklin close—there was even one called the confuse-the-customer close. All of that is so dead today. It's about understanding the customer's needs and challenges and leveraging your expertise and position of intelligence to help that customer *make the right decision*.

Pushing past no shouldn't be adversarial. You will face resistance even when people are interested and you know you have something they want and need. Your goal is about transference of belief. You believe your solution is the best. If you are truly trying to make customers see that you believe yes is the natural and logical conclusion to the process, be persistent and remember: Don't give up after the first signs of resistance, or the third, fourth, fifth. *Hang in there.*

PREPARE FOR IMPACT:
SELL PAST THE NO

- How can you maintain your solution is the right fit for their needs even when you encounter resistance without being adversarial?
- Are you comfortable with resistance and rejection?
- How skilled are you moving people past resistance?

13. Deadlines

Trustworthy people to do what they say they are going to do, when they say they're going to do it *every single time*. Don't miss deadlines—and if you are going to, be honest and let people know in advance that you need more time.

This is exactly what didn't happen when Ryan hired a brilliant, creative guy to support an important project and almost cost them their biggest consulting client at the time. The guy Ryan partnered with was a genius and delivered amazing work, but he never met a deadline he couldn't break, whether the clients' *or* his own. He *never* delivered when he said he would. "Sure, I can get that to you next week," he would say to clients. Then next week comes and . . . nothing. Not a word to us or the client. No, "Hey, I know we said next week, but could we have extra time to deliver something better?" There isn't a company in the world that wouldn't allow more time to get a better deliverable, even on deadline. Instead, Ryan and Lynn, his business manager, were constantly calling clients and apologizing for the company when she was really making excuses for this one guy. "We had such a great relationship with our clients, and now we had angst," Lynn remembers. "It didn't matter that this guy was brilliant. The process of dealing with him was awful, and it all came down to his unwillingness to carefully manage expectations around when he could produce and deliver when he promised—or tell us when he couldn't."

All this person needed to say was, "Hey, I need some time to get this right, and if it's okay I'll send a finished product next week. If you'd like to see the progress we made so far, I could send you what we have now." Instead, he made a promise and underdelivered. Working that way, you'll eventually lose the client and the relationship. This disrespect and disregard for the expectations cost them more than sleep. Because even when the work product was great, the experience of getting to the end was miserable.

To be clear, all the things we laid out here are an epidemic, not limited to one person or industry. Plenty of people and companies promise to deliver something faster than they know they can to win the business or simply because it sounds good. Someone sells the customer on what could be done and then tells the internal team to make it happen. Suddenly it's chaos as everyone scrambles to move things around to deliver on the promise to the customer. Maybe this does win them the business and make them look good, but eventually those actions begin to wear down customers and colleagues. It may be tempting to promise everything and then destroy yourself and the people around you to try to live up to those expectations. But it simply isn't a sound or sustainable strategy. In the long run, everyone loses. And clients that lose with you don't come back.

PREPARE FOR IMPACT:
DEADLINES

- How are you clear and consistent with what you deliver to and expect from others?
- How are you adept at turning problems into opportunities that improve relationships?

14. Follow-Up

For Chad, the difference between following up a no and letting it go was hundreds of millions of dollars and a new sales division for

> **80% of sales require five follow-up calls after the meeting; 94% of sales reps give up after one follow-up.[9]**

Legends Hospitality Management. That sales division at Legends took off only after Chad *failed* to get an important piece of business but continued to follow up.

Legends started as a concession company—a partnership between the Dallas Cowboys and the New York Yankees, along with Goldman Sachs, to offer a higher standard of food and beverage at the teams' new stadiums. It evolved to add a division that provided the industry with outsourced sales capabilities for tickets, premium seats, naming rights, and corporate sponsorships for dozens of teams and organizations in college and professional sports and beyond sports at other attractions worldwide, like at One World Trade Center in New York City.

The first Legends client was the 49ers, but that relationship was logical. They were an NFL team having a hard time getting public funding and their stadium built. They needed to do exactly what the Cowboys did at AT&T Stadium. So Chad still questioned if there was a next client. "I was putting a lot of pressure on myself because I was holding a lot of people back who had worked on the Cowboys' project to see if we could create this business rather than move them up or out to their next career steps. I told them not to take another job exactly when they would have a lot of value in the marketplace. Then the Rose Bowl decided to build a premium seating tower with suites and club seats. The City of Pasadena owns and operates the Rose Bowl, and they really didn't have a sales team. They asked people to come in and pitch that service, and we did. And we ended up *not* winning the deal. I was devastated. There went all the momentum. I questioned the business even more after that."

Chad thought, *Maybe we just do the 49ers project and move on.* But he still didn't stop following up. "The general manager at the Rose Bowl was really gracious in letting us down and explaining why we didn't win, so I kept communicating with him. I sent him five or six emails, explaining why we would be the best fit but never saying he was wrong. One time I emailed when I found someone working for another organization in LA who would have been perfect to run the Rose Bowl project for us. I knew he would have joined us if we had won the business, and I told the Rose Bowl GM that. Soon after that, the GM called me to say he was having a hard time coming to financial terms with the company he chose and asked if I could fly out there to talk. We inked the deal on that trip, and Legends sales division took off from there."

PREPARE FOR IMPACT:
FOLLOW-UP

- How and when do you follow up after an initial meeting?
- How do you follow up in a way that the prospect who told you no never forgets you?
- Name the biggest deal you lost in the last twelve months: How many times have you been in touch with that customer since?

---

15. Correspondence

This step was written when snail mail was king, but it's even more underserved today when we have so many ways to stay in touch— which is precisely why it stands out when you take the time to do it

> **Handwritten notes have a 99% open rate.**[10]

properly! Be honest: Can you really say a handwritten note doesn't mean something more to you and the person who receives it, whether in business or in general?

The process starts at first contact: Follow up meetings and calls with written correspondence—almost everyone you talk to should get a note or an email. These notes serve as reminders that you are committed to earning customers' business and serving their interests when the current vendor or person makes a mistake or falls out of favor, like Chad and the Rose Bowl business.

That said, some notes *must* be about more than selling. Hand-written notes of gratitude are a great way to show people you care and are thankful for not only their business but also who they are. Send them for no reason at all. Send notes for no other reason than that you saw something that made you think of them. Ryan sends clients notes with a book he thinks would be useful or interesting to them or explains something they think they should be doing. "I read this book and thought of you . . ." What better way to show you are thinking about clients and that you understand them. That you care about their success. That you are willing to take the time to convey all these things in words. That brings you closer to them.

Next time you come across a book or a story on something you *know* a person—anyone, not just a client or customer—would appreciate, don't just email a link. Send it with a note explaining why. That type of effort goes a long way, especially during the quiet period of a decision cycle.

PREPARE FOR IMPACT:
CORRESPONDENCE

- When was the last time you sent a note just because you were thinking of someone?
- When was the last time you just wrote a letter to say thanks?
- How does receiving a handwritten note or other gesture of appreciation make you feel?

16. Customer Service

Today's customers are more informed, sophisticated, and their expectations continue to evolve for customization, personalization, speed, and efficiency wherever they go. As a result, customer experience has become as important as, or even more important than, quality of product and service as the driver of value in today's economy. Salesforce's "State of Marketing Report" noted that expectations for great experience continue to rise: "84 percent of customers say the experience a company provides is as important as its products and services."[11] They'll even pay more for it. PricewaterhouseCoopers (PwC) research on the future of customer experience revealed that 73 percent of customers point to experience as an important factor in their purchasing decisions—and that experience, more than product or price, determines loyalty to the brand and leads to more referrals. PwC's warning was dire for those who fail to understand this: 59 percent of customers will walk away after several bad experiences. And what did 80 percent of customers say were two of the most important elements of a positive customer experience? Knowledgeable and friendly service (step 7 and this step together).[12]

58% of consumers and 77% of business buyers feel that technology has changed their expectations of how companies should interact with them.[13]

Human connection still matters both during and *after* the sale. After you acquire a customer, it's the way you seize the opportunity to customize and personalize the experience and deliver more value beyond the transaction or agreement. If you don't take care of your customer, somebody else will.

Ryan always says that if your work product is an A, but your service is a D, you are a C in terms of value to your customer and their experience. Because customer service today is all about the *experience*.

When Ryan does events for companies that have a unique brand and a physical location, like Five Guys, Tiffany's, or Lowe's, he will often come onstage wearing something from the company—for example, the Five Guys red golf shirt uniform, the vest service members wear at Lowe's, a tie bar from Tiffany's—to make the clients feel like Ryan is a part of the team. Ryan also offers *for no extra fee* to bring a photographer and a video crew to a store location for a day to capture assets and content, interview managers, and see and speak to customers. This gives him and the client a deep perspective that he incorporates into his keynote or training. "The clients can't believe I'm willing to do that," says Ryan. "No one had ever done that for them before. Yeah, it costs me a couple of thousand dollars and an extra day of time, but it has created such a competitive differentiation by stacking value. Now they want me to do more work, and I have a case study that I can leverage to demonstrate value to other clients. It also elevates both the experience and impact I can create from the learning."

For Chad and his team selling season tickets, customer service has evolved way beyond the days of just focusing on what happens after the sale is made, how the tickets are delivered, and stopping by customers' seats to do some public relations. It combines people analytics with that human touch.

"When I worked for the Tampa Bay Lightning, we were in last place, but at the end of the game, all the salespeople would stand out there and thank the fans. 'You guys suck!' they would scream back . . . and worse," Chad recalls. "But we took it and kept on thanking them because we were genuinely grateful. Today the level of sophistication for managing customer relationships goes way beyond stopping by seats and thanking people after games. It's about how we handle and understand service and the overall customer experience. We use point trackers, focus groups, and analytics. We don't just script a stadium experience like we did in Cleveland; we *study* it. We have dedicated service teams. Still, the point is the same: the relationship doesn't end after the sale is made, so neither should the service that customer gets from the organization at all levels. We have always encouraged that sales reps stay involved with customers and not hand them off to the service team. How much they do it is up to them. They know the more you stay involved with your customers, the more business that leads to because of referrals and upsells in the future."

Problems are often opportunities to exceed expectations and deepen relationships. Nothing worse than someone who has no empathy for what you've been going through and tells you there's nothing they can do. Because it's never the problem that people remember; it's the way it gets resolved. Addressing a problem the right way up front strengthens the relationship. When you are consumed by problem resolution, people are overwhelmed by the response. It deepens their loyalty and respect—and can lead to more, not lost, business.

"People appreciate and value that sense of urgency and immediacy—the transparency, candor, and effort," says Ryan. "Customers understand that things go wrong in business. That's life. People are a little more relaxed about that when they know you are aware of it, trust you to deal with it, and know you have the best intentions and their interests in mind. That's critical to a long-term business partnership. Those are the magic moments. If everything is fine and minimum expectations were met in an everyday transaction, it's not memorable. Even if the outcome is great, if the experience getting to the outcome is miserable, then you are in trouble. When you exceed expectations and blow someone's mind through the experience, you create a customer for life and a catalyst for growth."

Take the time to audit your customer experience. The easiest way to start is to use the questions that follow that Ryan developed to audit his customer experiences.

PREPARE FOR IMPACT:
CUSTOMER SERVICE

- What are you doing to make it easy to do business with you?
- What are you doing well?
- What could you do differently or better?
- What's worth investing in to change?
- How can we take the extra step to customize the experience?
- What happens when a customer lands on your website? Emails your office?
- Calls or leaves a message on voicemail?
- What happens after the sale is complete? How can you provide what Ryan and his team call "aftercare?"
- Where can you add value and deepen the relationship and continue to differentiate you from your competitors?
- How can you add more value to every customer touch point, online and offline?

17. Know Your Competition

Back in the day, we kept actual files of competitive intelligence on competitors and their top clients and prospects—actual files with hard copies of any documentation that could be procured from the marketplace, such as proposals, sales literature, collateral, and rate cards—that might help us understand how they position themselves and improve our ability to compete. Today those files are digital, but the point is the same: We make it our business to know everything about who or what we are competing against. We research everything to uncover what they do and study all of it to benchmark ourselves.

36% of buyers say deals are immediately killed if sellers don't understand their competitors' products and services.[14]

There is always competition, often head-to-head competition, for the biggest deals. Those requests for proposals (RFPs) cost money, resources, and dozens, if not hundreds, of team hours. Which is why if you have done the work of the previous steps and built a relationship with a potential customer, you can get answers to important questions, use them to your advantage, and be more efficient and targeted in your approach: Why is this RFP coming out? What happened? Who is the organization using now? What's most important to them?

"In my ad agency days, we were deeply educated on our current and potential customers and then tried to develop relationships with them so we could get answers to questions like these in competitive selling situations," says Ryan. "And if we didn't have someone on the inside of a potential account, we used our current clients. We'd go to our best customers, especially our best new customers, and use them as a resource to understand why they selected us, what they loved, and who else they were considering and had worked with previously. What did you like about who we beat out? How did they respond? This helps us get to know our customers and deepens the relationship with them. It shows them that we are still in the game and want to serve them. That we still care about the business while we have it, not the next sale."

Ryan also uses clients like Chad as a resource. He hires other keynote speakers, like Simon Sinek and Gary Vaynerchuk. He finds out everything that happened from the minute those people called his team's offices: Who answered? What did they say? How long did it take them to get back to you? Who sold you on the contract? When did you first talk to the speakers themselves? How did they prepare? How many people helped? Was someone traveling with them? What did they do? What kind of gum did they chew? Ryan wants to get every ounce of information to understand what others who are successful are doing differently and find out where we can improve to better serve his customers in the future. That intelligence informs your approach and helps to develop your own unique value proposition.

It is just as important to find out why customers left and went with another person, product, or service. It's not trying to sell past the no at that point. It's about a deep desire for more information so we can learn and grow. How did we lose to these guys? Are we too expensive? Were they looking for a different experience? Different services? More skill level or experience in the industry? Is our positioning messed up? Did we miss when explaining what we offer? You need the answers to questions like these to better articulate your value proposition. Don't get complacent. You can't be afraid to ask the questions and do the work that gets you this information.

"Too many people, when they get or lose a piece of business and get that final no, let this quest for knowledge go," Ryan continues. "Yeah, maybe what we find out is nothing we could have dealt with. If they wanted different expertise or insight and we're not the right fit, that's okay. But more often we learn what we are not doing right or simply could have done better. We can't get better without getting the information that helps us grow."

Start by reviewing your competitors' positioning, news, proposals, and pitch decks, if you can get your hands on them—know what they know. Find out how and where they make their connections. Attend their events. Talk to the people who have worked for them.

PREPARE FOR IMPACT:
KNOW YOUR COMPETITION

- Why should somebody do business with you?
- Who and what are you up against when getting someone to choose you or what you're selling?
- What can you do that your competition cannot—that the customer cannot live without?

18. Know Your Clients

You need to talk like your customers and understand their world. The more you know about what customers are trying to accomplish, what their challenges are, and embrace customer success as your own success, the more effective you can be in orchestrating value around your deliverables—and get them to stop focusing on price. Remember: Customers don't buy on price; they default to price in the absence of value and a quality experience. Salespeople help make that happen by understanding their customers and expertly delivering a differentiated and compelling experience that drives results and creates customers for life. The more you correlate what you offer to their desired outcomes, the better servant you have been—and the higher the probability that you're going to get invited back and/or referred for more work based on the relationships you have developed.

When the Dallas Cowboys built the Star, the team's corporate headquarters and practice facility in Frisco, Texas, Chad and his team started upselling sponsorship opportunities to existing customers. He called his contact at one sponsor who had been working with the team for about ten years at AT&T Stadium, and he basically said, "I'm in." This was a big annual deal Chad was pitching and a completely new project. Huge deals like that involve several conversations, an evaluation by the client, agency involvement, presentations, and even negotiations. This client said that would all have to happen, but he wanted Chad to know he was

> Only 13% of customers believe salespeople can understand their needs.[15]

in. He said, "The way you guys operate, whatever you tell me the deal is, it's going to be ten times better than that because that's how you have delivered for us so far. So let's review and talk about details."

"That's not normal, but it was gratifying," says Chad. "His trust was founded on how well we knew them, which meant they felt they knew us. We had customized and delivered value for what we knew they needed and wanted, which is what we try to do for every client by making sure we never get complacent and stop working to know what they need and want."

A great way to get to know your clients—even early in your career—is to invite them to the table and create a client advisory board (CAB) for yourself and/or your team and organization. In our experience, clients are never shy about telling you what they need, what they'll buy from you, and where they are going. A CAB simply formalizes this process and allows customers to offer insight and expertise on a regular basis. A CAB invites them to collaborate and coinnovate with you, validating them as experts and deepening partnerships. This helps you evolve in your business in lockstep with what matters to your customers and naturally creates new revenue opportunities.

Start your CAB now by picking up the phone and calling three or four of your best clients. Say you respect their opinions and thought leadership and ask them questions about their business, the marketplace, or issues you are having. After a couple of those calls, ask if it would be okay if once a quarter you reached out and used them as sounding boards. Within a year, you will be so much more informed and know your clients better than ever.

PREPARE FOR IMPACT:
KNOW YOUR CLIENTS

- How do you make the world better for your customers?
- What does success look like for them?
- How do your customers define a successful outcome with you?
- Who should serve on your CAB?

19. Assume the Sale

When making a presentation, don't just sell the benefits. Act as if you know the person is going to buy. It should simply be the natural and logical conclusion of an expertly managed sales process. You want to make people feel that if they don't buy and buy from you—*now*—they will be missing out on a big opportunity and imply subtly that if they don't it will be a mistake.

"Having people come to the arena looking at suites for the Cavs went beyond selling the benefits," says Chad. "We would assume the sale. We would start by asking for objections up front, saying, 'Obviously, you have made a decision to come down here today. You've thought about what we are going to discuss. What would prevent you today from making a positive decision about moving forward with a suite?' Then we'd sit there and listen to the objections up front, which we prepared for from practicing and anticipated from asking questions. Someone might say, 'I have heard they are pretty expensive,' and we would say, 'Assume we can find something in your budget.' All we were doing was finding out where they were at. That gets you to a place where you can not only ask for the order at any time but also start working on the details of the sale."

But be careful not to offend; be confident but not arrogant. Remember: Assuming the sale is about putting yourself in an optimistic mindset. You believe something is right for the customer and simply need to transfer that belief. Just like good athletes visualize what success will look like in a game, good salespeople visualize sales discussions going their way. Potential customers feel this energy, and it makes them feel more confident making a decision.

PREPARE FOR IMPACT:
ASSUME THE SALE

- When was the last time you succeeded or failed to act as if you had the sale? What was the result?
- How do you get the customer to believe what you believe?

20. Sell Yourself

Life is sales: We're all competing for time, attention, and resources to move or advance our ideas, thoughts, opinions, beliefs. We're all trying to convince people to see things our way. And it isn't just salespeople with customers. Presenting your ideas to achieve buy-in and get someone to act is a part of life. This goes way beyond references and facts about who else bought from you and how much. You need those things, for sure, but don't forget the power of stories to frame them, the work you've done, and who you are. Tell the story of how you or what you're selling solved a problem or met the needs of a similar company or person. Ask your best customers to participate in outcomes-based case studies and embed that into your go-to-market strategy—then present it through a story. But don't just do this reactively. Make sure you leverage every tool, technology, and asset you have.

Anyone who has been to the Star, the Dallas Cowboys world headquarters in Frisco, Texas, knows how the team uses its entire campus—from the hotel to the many restaurants and stores—to tell and share its story with TVs streaming the Cowboys' greatest hits and a turf field open to anyone. You can't help but be drawn in the moment you arrive, whether as a fan or a potential customer of the team. The whole campus is the team's front desk.

As someone selling himself, Ryan doesn't have a campus, but he does have a portfolio of client case studies and ideas to leverage. That's why Ryan has a YouTube channel, an active social media presence, a newsletter, and constantly writes and publishes articles. He doesn't hold back on content either. "Give all your best ideas away for free, and the world will respond" is one of his mantras. Ideas may be a dime a dozen; there is only one Ryan.

"I have been sharing content online for over a decade now, and it has changed my life and my business. Good salespeople get the idea of getting found. I call them micromarketers," Ryan says. "My whole business is built around getting referred or getting found. That's a global statement—literally. The largest bank in Romania found me on a Google search and hired me to give a speech to their top two hundred executives in Bucharest. That happens at least once a week. Someone will call and say, 'Hey, we are looking for a speaker for a sales conference, and we found you.' This was true even after conferences went virtual during the pandemic. I was the opening keynote speaker for Eufora International salons because they saw a video of me talking about my experience in a coffee shop. The power of that video getting sixty-five million views and all the energy we put into content marketing is worth it. It takes time and investment, but it makes sales easier."

Just don't let your dedication to getting found discount the importance of making a great first impression when you talk face-to-face. You want to show up prepared. You can even have fun with it. Ryan's business manager, Lynn, was meeting with a potential client, Memorial Blood Centers, and Ryan told her that she had to give blood first.

"What?"

"Walk in wearing short sleeves, with the Band-Aid and gauze thingy showing on your arm."

"What are you talking about?"

"Go give blood and then go in there and tell them you donated blood and then come to the appointment."

To this day, if you said to Lynn "blood for business," she would laugh. But of the ten people who called on the Memorial Blood Centers that week, how many of them did that? It's important to remember that the customer always buys you first.

PREPARE FOR IMPACT:
SELL YOURSELF

- How do people find you, and how does what they find sell you?
- How does your presence create additional value during the decision process or cycle?
- If you were on the other end of your presentation, would you buy you?

21. Enthusiasm

A sale is simply the transference of belief for what you're selling to the buyer, including *yourself*. The best salespeople get you to believe. Their enthusiasm conveys this belief and excitement. If you can't get excited about what you're selling or doing in any situation, then why would you expect people you're selling to?

Selling is psychologically and emotionally demanding and mandates grit and resilience. You have your training, you get all fired up, and then you go out and sell. And then you get rejected, over and over again. Even the best of the best are going to have the energy sucked out of them when that happens. How you handle that is absolutely going to impact your future success, perhaps more than anything else. Don't lose control of your emotions, get frustrated, and throw in the towel. Don't try to fake it till you make it. Terrible advice. Face it until you make it! Top producers anticipate obstacles and respond with intention and resolve. Use your energy to change the dynamic and get yourself fully engaged. Let positive energy flow over the phone, in meetings, and throughout your office—even on social media, in emails, and anything you write. Even when you're in a slump. Especially when you are in a slump.

If your enthusiasm disappears along with your energy, then you are going to stay down. You have to clear your mind and sell that next thing.

In trainings, Ryan often plays a recording of a cold call and asks what the person did and did not do well. "The bad calls always get the same reaction: 'He's not very positive,' or, 'She doesn't have a lot of energy,' which reads as no enthusiasm. Then we role-play. I make them act like a person with no enthusiasm—low energy, depressed, blaming everyone for your bad day, exhausted. They are all slumping, heads down. I say, 'Now act confident. Act like a badass. Act like you believe deeply with every cell in your body and you have the right idea in your chair. How does that person look and feel?' They're standing up, waving their arms, moving around. Now they know how to create energy and enthusiasm on command. That knowledge is power. You have that ability to access limitless reserves of energy and enthusiasm. You just have to decide!"

If you need a boost, turn to a teammate for help. The people around you can give you that energy back. That's the foundation of this and the teamwork step—everyone working together to lift everyone up, encourage each other, and share ideas. If you see your teammates' heads down and slumping, you know you need to help them turn around.

PREPARE FOR IMPACT:
ENTHUSIASM

- How did your enthusiasm show up today?
- How are you protecting and preserving your energy?
- How are you facing the truth and doing something about it?

---

22. Relationships

Selling is about earning commitment. A commitment has shared responsibilities and mutually agreed upon outcomes. But relationships go beyond the sale. The quality of all aspects of your life, not just your sales success, is based on the quality of your relationships. Your ability to build meaningful relationships with your customers, team, bosses, friends, and family is critical to your success, your career trajectory, your ability to lead an organization, and your happiness.

Having a relationship means thinking about customers as people, not prospects, and treating them as people, not commodities. How you treat

> **89% of buyers say the salespeople they do business with are "trusted advisors."**[16]

others reflects how they will treat you—and help you get referred. It's about who you know and who knows you well enough to want to work with you and refer others to work with you as well. If you're not getting referred and getting found, you're relying on antiquated, interruption-based sales tactics that are going to have diminishing returns in the future—that is, cold calls. Cold calls are a low-probability conversion and often a waste of time for even the best salespeople. You want to sell to people who already have an investment in you. Who know about you or, in Ryan's case, have seen him working somewhere. It's not enough for the customer to be satisfied. We want customers to be evangelists who help us create growth by telling somebody else why they do business with us. For that, we need relationships.

"My whole thesis on speaking is based on my whole sales experience: one keynote needs to generate two more qualified opportunities," says Ryan. "For example, I did a workshop at the NBA's sales and marketing conference, and I got a call from the NBA's law firm to keynote their partners conference on a referral from the league. That's gold. Now, my business is different from Chad's. He has to have a bunch of people banging out calls, and so do many of the companies I work with. But the best way to make those sales easier and the fastest way for companies to grow, especially small businesses, is to generate referrals founded on the relationships you built from delivering a remarkable experience."

Simply put, if you're focused on the transaction alone, you'll never build relationships with your customers and clients and turn them into your evangelists. Instead of focusing on how to be successful, focus on how you can be helpful.

PREPARE FOR IMPACT:
RELATIONSHIPS

- Beyond the sale, how committed are you to the success of the customers and clients you serve?
- What is your process for generating referrals?

23. Goals

Most sales and marketing jobs revolve around quotas and goals of some kind. But few professionals who work in those businesses set those goals for themselves. After Ryan heard Jim Rohn speak, he walked out of the presentation with a workbook and began to take notes that night, starting with something he had never done or been told to do before: he wrote out his personal goals for the months, year, and years ahead.

"I still have it!" Ryan says. "Before that night, I was just trying to survive. Jim Rohn changed my thinking. One meaningful goal could change the trajectory of my life. I knew I needed to take the time to set that goal. I thought, *Anyone can be a salesperson, but I decided I was going to be a top producer.* Even though I hadn't made a sale and was about to get fired, I decided that within the next year I would be the number-one account executive in the company. I looked at that goal every morning. It fueled my increase in activity and competency. It was hard work, but I did it. Every goal I have set since has been just as meaningful and worthwhile to achieve. With each new goal I achieved, I got to define *success* for myself and how I wanted to live in the future. That freedom of choice is beautiful. That's what I wanted Chad and everyone who works with me to become obsessed with achieving for themselves."

Where's your plan? Decide what you want, set goals, embrace the right habits, monitor progress, self-assess, solicit regular feedback, adapt, and enjoy the ride!

PREPARE FOR IMPACT:
GOALS

- How often do you revisit the goals and plans you laid out in the past?
- Have you decided what you want to accomplish today, this week, month, and year? Write that down and refer to it often.

---

24. Teamwork

Be a team player—the person who shares, takes on extra projects, and steps up to help. Someone *will* take notice. It's amazing how the opposite approaches—politics, silos, hypercompetitiveness—create environments rife with negativity, issues, and unnecessary tension among people.

Chad learned quickly that the teamwork expected of the players did not extend to the organization as a whole. "When I was a sales rep, I was third or fourth on the sales board, killing myself for not being number one. One of my bosses came up to me and said, 'Hey, man, you're not number one on the board. Why aren't you number one?' Do you think in that environment I wanted the two or three people ahead of me to be having any success? No, I hoped something horrible happened to them. I had it hammered into me that was the way it was in an ultracompetitive environment, and I had to be the best. But here's the thing: In environments where everybody is pitted against each other, not celebrating and helping each other, those are the environments filled with negativity, insecurity, and blame. My key learning from my experience was how *not* to create that kind of environment when I moved into

> Teamwork and collaboration increase company sales by 27%.[17]

leadership, had some control of the culture and how I interacted with the people working for me, and could abide by this step."

It *is* possible to have success and be happy for the people around us. It's also possible not to buy into the negativity and yet still have some healthy competition that drives everyone to be their best. Contributing to a high-functioning team is actually way more fulfilling and fun.

When Ryan and Lynn worked together at the ad agency, Ryan was her manager but also had a sales quota to reach. So they created internal competition and channeled that into something positive. "We created our own World Series of Cold Calling. We would go hard for three hours, and the one who got the most appointments won a soda or lunch. We made it fun and productive. We would get more appointments in that three-hour window than we did all week long. We pushed each other just like Chad and I did and still do today. It was healthy competition based on mutual respect, not jealousy and territorialism."

In fact, one of the biggest deals Lynn ever put together at the agency was the Mayo Clinic, and they were Ryan's prospect for five years. One day Ryan walked into Lynn's office and said, "I'm getting nowhere with these people. I want you to try." She did more than try. She got the business. It wasn't about the credit. It was about what was best for the business and ultimately the customer. About being a great teammate. You must put your success in the service of that and the success of the organization, not yourself alone.

The questions that follow are not easy to ask and answer honestly, especially if you're in a competitive environment that demands results of any kind, and we all have our moments. But they are essential to understanding what "being a good teammate" means—and should mean to you.

PREPARE FOR IMPACT:
TEAMWORK

- Are you genuinely happy for other people on the team to have success?
- How do you use the spirit of healthy competition to push each other and compete?
- How do you contribute and support the success of the team?

---

25. Difficult Prospects

The most difficult prospects can be the best customers. They challenge you to think about your approach and test what you know, the services and products you offer, and your resilience. The more we are pushed by clients, the better we become for the next ones. We often find they make our entire business better.

"I was on the short list to win a large contract and had to fly to NYC for a final pitch on how I would approach the client's business," Ryan recalls. "They were *tough* in that meeting. They asked for a preview of what I would do. They picked apart my content and forced me to defend and advocate for my position. They challenged whether what I was presenting was actionable enough for their audience. None of it was personal. It was about getting what's right for their business, not mine. All that pushed me to solidify my answers and my performance. My business is stronger, and I am better for it. What I went through I can bring to bear on other customers."

Many people don't see it the way Ryan did. When they encounter a challenging client who pushes them to answer tough questions, prove their concepts, and provide more data, they fight back instead of creating better processes around their approaches that help them with the next ten clients. Meeting their challenges—even when you don't close the deal—helps you understand why other similar prospects might not be biting, pushes you to keep being better, and evolves what you need to do so you can satisfy them or someone like them the next time.

Difficult prospects also force you to expand, raise your game, and improve. You should *expect* and be *excited* for the challenge of those situations. They make you better, and when you get better nobody can take that from you.

PREPARE FOR IMPACT:
DIFFICULT PROSPECTS

- How do you respond to a customer when they challenge you?
- How have challenging prospects and customers stretched you to grow?

---

26. Mentoring

The 30 Steps grew out of a mentoring relationship between Ryan and Chad. Ryan did for Chad what any good mentor does: inspires

> Research shows support from mentors has a significant impact on an individual's career and personal growth.[18]

you, stretches you, connects you, develops you, guides you, challenges you, holds you accountable, helps you when you're stuck, and provides you with a safe space to learn, grow, and cultivate your potential. At any point in your career, it's easy to get overwhelmed and feel like you are making moves that might be a big misstep. A mentor can help you explore what you want to get out of your career.

Ryan likes to find mentors who are a little bit further down the road than he was with Chad to prepare for the journey he aspires to take. "I want to ask my mentors, 'What mistake did you make years ago that you regret today? How do you balance work and life? Looking back, what would you do differently? When you have a mentor who has been where you want to go, you receive an incredible gift of perspective. One of my mentors, Larry Flick, told me what he enjoys most today is 'connecting the dots, figuring out where the future is, and helping people navigate there sooner than anybody else.' He likes creating opportunities in which people can grow and achieve their dreams by working with and for him, so he prioritizes coaching and mentoring. He isn't waiting to leave a legacy. He is leading a legacy right now by helping people around him succeed. That has been hugely influential to me as a leader."

Don't have a mentor? Find one! Who you spend time with affects your perspective, motivation, and how you experience the world—and it affects your future. Think about what you want to learn and the skills you need to cultivate. Write them down. Now ask yourself: Who can you access in your own life that can provide that support? Why do you admire and respect them so much? Pick someone in your organization, industry, network, or community that exemplifies everything you want to become.

Next, ask that person to go have a drink and talk about how that person got there. Use the steps you've mastered to convince that person to be your mentor: know who they are, be professional, ask questions, show enthusiasm, sell yourself, and then ask for the sale. If all that fails, hire a business coach who has insight, wisdom, and expertise that you do not. Ryan did that early on and felt it was the best investment in himself he could make, which is why he still has a coach today—and always will. Can't afford a coach? You don't have to be mentored by someone you know or even someone living. Do what we did at the start of our careers: immerse yourself in the books and other work of the people you admire.

PREPARE FOR IMPACT:
MENTORING

- Do you have a mentor?
- Where do you go to learn?

27. Surround Yourself with Successful People

Jobs, employees, and life in general change as we grow. Great bosses and mentors are important but only get you so far. No matter where you are in your career, we all need people who are more than mentors—people you can share everything with. Having people who push you to be your best self and compete—and even have fun doing it the way we do for each other.

The origin of this step dates to the first time Ryan saw Jim Rohn and heard one of his most enduring principles: "You are the average of the five people you spend the most time with." Rohn made Ryan realize who you surround yourself with is perhaps the single most important decision you make. Success and good habits are contagious, as are negative ones. Hang out with people who bring you up.

"In the fraternity, Chad and I were lifted up by our brotherhood, and it changed the course of my college career and our relationship," Ryan says. "I needed to audit my circle and spend time with people who would help me become a better version of myself. I'm still learning, growing, and benefitting from that shift. Today I have three business partners, and we do more than collaborate on our company, ImpactEleven. Once a quarter, we do a practice review and audit of one of the partner's thought-leadership practices. My partners are deeply skilled, with insight gained from building multimillion-dollar businesses around thought leadership. I get to walk through my positioning, strategy, and structure for them. Then they offer candid feedback, asking questions and making suggestions. It is humbling in the most beneficial way, and I'm grateful for it. I am growing exponentially because of their counsel, and the truth is, we really are better together."

If you want to raise your own capability and continue making forward progress, it pays to audit your circle. If you already have informal mentors and friends helping you, Ryan suggests expanding and formalizing it by creating what he calls a personal board of directors (PBOD)—a group of carefully vetted advisors whose judgment you respect and who lend invaluable expertise and competency. Ryan has his partners, but he relies on his PBOD. Chad is on it, as is Ryan's life coach, his financial advisor, and his business manager, Lynn. Ryan calls on his PBOD similar to the way an organization calls on its board of directors: for their guidance and insights to help him make more informed strategic decisions and achieve his goal of building a better business and a more enriching life that makes meaningful contributions to others.

Having a PBOD can be incredibly useful for your business. But as you think about who to put on your board, don't just think of family and friends. Your family and friends may have great insights, but they may not have the expertise you need to build your business. Instead, think of people you respect whose insights you can learn from to get you and/or your business to their next iteration.

PREPARE FOR IMPACT:

SURROUND YOURSELF WITH SUCCESSFUL PEOPLE

- Who are the people in your life who support you, celebrate your successes, and push you to compete and be your best?
- How do you like your average of your five people?
- Who would you invite to your personal board of directors?

---

28. Don't Break Promises

Don't undo the work of the other twenty-six steps that came before this one by making promises you can't or don't intend to keep, and never overpromise and underdeliver, especially if you're trying to close a sale. That's a relationship killer and all too common a mistake that sellers make. No matter how badly you want to earn the commitment, fight the desire to stretch too far to get to yes. Be honest about what you can and cannot deliver, and if you can't deliver and you created an expectation that you could, you need to call that customer and immediately explain why.

In competitive situations, we all can be tempted to say and be everything to move a customer to a place of decision. But you must balance that with what is realistic within the context of your own organization. Why be dishonest about what your capabilities are? Better to overdeliver by not promising the moon than falling short in the client or customer's eyes.

Of course, we all make mistakes. Stuff happens that forces us to break a promise or go back on our word. When it does, you need to call that customer immediately and explain why. That's when you realize the power of transparency and the importance of delivering bad news when it happens quickly, up front, and honestly in strengthening that trust, not to mention earning respect and deepening the relationship. This is true in every aspect of our lives. Too often, however, we see people hesitant to do this because we are wired for comfort, not conflict, and because of fear—fear for what others will say, only to disappoint them more when they find out later and/or we can't solve the problem and deliver.

"I maintain it isn't the problem but the resolution the customer remembers," Ryan says. "It's important to have the willingness to confront this truth. I worked for someone whose default was to hide problems and bad news from the customer. 'We don't have to tell them everything.' It was cover up and cover your ass and a terrible way of doing business. It gave everyone anxiety that could have been mitigated or eliminated by picking up the phone and having a tough but honest conversation."

When you do have that conversation, however, you must come prepared with a resolution or understanding of what you can do that will blow the customer's mind or at least make them know you care about finding a solution. That will deepen the relationship, and people will appreciate the trust and the transparency even if they don't love the news.

Consider what happened to Chad at the Cowboys. His team had signed a contract for a major corporate event on the field for one thousand people and didn't realize until *after* they signed that they screwed up the calendar and double-booked. "I told the rep who had the relationship with the client to get them on the phone in my office," Chad recalls. "'We're just gonna call them right now?' he asked. Absolutely. We were going to call them and admit we had a major screwup, ask for a meeting, and start to work on an alternative. I knew they were going to be pissed, and they were. *Extremely* pissed. We let them vent. And once they vented, we went to work on how we were going to resolve it."

That time Chad took responsibility for delivering the news, but in leading by example, his rep understood that in the end the clients respect your straightforwardness—even if they need to vent first. Chad's rep learned to execute this step, and they ended up fixing the issue by moving the client's event to another, albeit less desirable, date and adding complementary elements to the event as a value add to make up for the change. The client ended up being very satisfied with the event and interaction with the organization. In the end, Chad's quick admission to their mistake, honest and up-front way of handling it, and the opportunity to create more value to fix it has resulted in a phenomenal relationship with that client—maybe even more than if that mistake had never happened.

But one last note: It can be just as much a mistake to underpromise and overdeliver. Much better to simply deliver more than the customer expected. Ryan manages to do this even though he and his partners offer the most comprehensive service level agreements (SLA) in his industry: twenty-one points that cover every nuance and detail offering pretty compelling differentiation of his company's services and experiences.

He knows delivery can be a source of competitive differentiation, and the SLA comes from a mindset of service and investing more to build a relationship.

PREPARE FOR IMPACT:
DON'T BREAK PROMISES

- How are you making promises you can legitimately and consistently deliver, no exceptions?
- How have you and the entire internal team aligned your delivering client expectations that get sold?
- How are you delivering on client expectations consistently?

---

29. One Final Call

At the end of the day, when you've had enough of a bad day and decide to pack it in, *stop*. Pick up the phone and make one more call. Make one more chance to touch base with a client or prospect and create some positive momentum that you can take with you when you go home. Try to end on a positive note and carry some momentum home and into the next day. It doesn't matter how you make that last call—phone, email, in person—just make it.

"I used to say to my people you can make five thousand phone calls. One of those calls could change your career," says Chad. "In my business, season-ticket sales are important, and if my last call sold two season tickets and that person seems to like me, I've seen where that can lead. That person bought two and then four and then he wanted his friends to go, so he referred them to me. Now it's twenty season tickets because of that. So, when you are mentally ready to shut down, just say, 'I'm going to make that one last call.' When you get a success story, you feel great. Every sale, every relationship starts somewhere. The whole point is, you just never know when that's going to happen. It could happen on that last call. That could be the one."

PREPARE FOR IMPACT:
ONE FINAL CALL

- When did you give one more rep? How did it turn out?
- How did the success (or failure) make you feel?

---

30. Exercise

Christmas Day 2019 was a warm-for-December morning in Cleveland when we came outside our mother's house. The annual Ice Run. The Ice Run is about three miles to the bottom of the development and back. By banging a right at the bottom, we can stretch the run to four miles. We approached with the same unspoken understanding we did the sprints that started chapter 1: This wasn't just a workout. The race was *on*.

"We going to go to the bottom and back, or are we doing the four-miler?" Ryan asked Chad as they stepped outside. He knew Chad drank a lot of wine on Christmas Eve and might be shaking off some cobwebs. He was right: If Chad had been alone, there is no way he would have run. But Ryan was ready, and he got dressed. There was no way Chad wanted to do four, but he wasn't giving anything away.

"Let's decide once we get to the bottom," Chad responded.

> 64% of Americans experience a boost in self-confidence and 67% experience increased productivity when they practice self-care.[19]

One hundred yards in, Chad was miserable. Nothing felt good. He had a headache. He knew then the only chance he had to make this a race was to have Ryan *think* that he felt good and hope Ryan was miserable as he was, gain a big lead, and limp into victory. As they approached the bottom, Chad picked up the pace to an extremely uncomfortable level. He got about ten yards ahead of Ryan, and then without saying a word banged the right for the four-miler, extending his lead to about twenty yards.

It almost worked.

Ryan considered conceding but kept going. Then he saw Chad slowing down and laboring a little. Ryan knew what he had to do: He inched forward and waited until he was close enough to pass him aggressively at the point where there wasn't too much race left. If he left too much road, and Chad was strong at the finish, he would lose. With about half a mile left, Ryan took him.

"He blew right past me, and I had nothing to give," says Chad. "I stopped running and walked some. I was so defeated. I was so pissed off."

"I broke his spirit. I took everything he had left."

"I took an L. It happens."

It does. As much as neither of us wanted to lose that (or any) race with each other, we have both arrived at a place in life where we know that there is something else beyond achievement, and we are never going to get there without practicing self-care, which is what Ryan would call this step today.

Part of the reason we have our competitions—spoken and unspoken—is to push us to take care of ourselves. The nature of balancing life and work means we often get into this space where we are traveling, entertaining, and eating out for days on end. For example, when Chad took a day off to start work on this book, he was coming off a stretch of thirty-four straight days during which he had at least one long meeting, ate food that was bad for him, and consumed alcohol.

Of course, what going all day means might look different post-pandemic for many of us by choice or by circumstance. There are fewer business professionals on the road for days on end. But Chad still rolls from meeting to meeting every day with the future of the people who work for him and millions of dollars seemingly always on the line. Ryan's pivot to digital from in-person presentations and then starting a new company meant something always needed to be done *now*. Phones are always on—heck, "everyone" expects them to be—just in case we're needed or need something. Social media demands we keep up. Family, kids, friendships, and relationships deserve our attention. So does that side hustle or perhaps some gig-economy work to pay the bills while working our way up. And didn't we just tell you to make that last call?

No matter your working conditions, you won't be able to enjoy your success or any of these things, let alone perform them to the best of your ability, if you fail to maintain a healthy lifestyle. In fact, the global pandemic only made this more essential by pinning us to our desks alone at home when we used to enjoy community and camaraderie and get in some steps walking the hall or airport terminals. The 2022 annual *Stress in America* report from the American Psychological Association found that 58 percent of Americans gained undesired weight since the start of the pandemic.[20]

So heed these words: Practice self-care all year long. Take care of yourself and respect your body. This includes sleep, mindfulness, diet, and exercise. Just move. Breathe. Take a brisk walk for fifteen minutes. Leave the phone and find a partner if you can and push each other to do it daily while you have a conversation. You will burn calories, but more importantly have more energy, see things more clearly, feel better about yourself, reduce stress, and be happier. All that translates directly to your ability to deal with adversity and to your attitude toward work and life. You might even learn something and deepen a relationship while you're at it.

PREPARE FOR IMPACT:
EXERCISE

- What have you done this week to improve your body and your mind?
- How is stress, burnout, or exhaustion negatively affecting your life?
- How can you practice quality self-care?

CHAPTER 4

STEPPING INTO LEADERSHIP

HERE'S HOW RYAN RECALLS his initial jump from sales representative to sales manager: "I wanted people to do it exactly the way I did it: My way was to come into the office at six in the morning and grind. 'How can you not be here at six a.m.? What's wrong with you?' I would say that to someone just out of college and to a mom who has three kids at home. To help me lead this way, I hired two regional guys who on first impression reminded me of me, and in short order they both flamed out. It was a rough start."

Ryan realized he had figured out how to be the best sales rep in the company: do the 30 Steps, and you will dominate the field. But the idea of leading or managing people, building relationships with them, and helping them achieve their own success? "I had ego and self-esteem issues, insecurity, and perfectionist issues. I didn't get the difference between getting results and developing talent. I probably should have been on the chopping block *again*."

To solve his problem, Ryan knew what he had to do: Work on

himself. He had to step back into the learning lane and become a student of leadership. That's when he came across *Don't Fire Them, Fire Them Up* by Frank Pacetta.

Fired Up

Unlike Jim Rohn, Frank Pacetta wasn't a towering figure on the leadership speaker circuit. He was a regional Ohio guy with a Brooklyn accent who rose through the ranks at Xerox. When Ryan read his book and listened to the book on tape, he was floored. "This guy was unbelievable. He told stories like no one else. The title alone shifted my mindset. When I started, I wanted to fire everybody. Frank set me straight. He told a story about when he was young how he got thrown into leadership and decided to keep everyone and give them a chance instead of firing them. He took his office from worst to first in a year by getting the troops to follow him. His people had fun. They loved coming to work every day. I had to learn to fire my team up the same way—maximize their potential to be the best they could be, in their own way."

Which is why when Chad was promoted into management, the first book Ryan sent him was Frank's.

"Frank was our hero," Chad says. "We'd imitate him on the phone, taking turns telling his stories word for word. When we had problems or needed to fire someone, we would ask, 'What would Frank do?' His character, his values, the way he would prioritize his family and cared about his people above all . . . he was a great leader because he was a great man who cared about people. He understood selfish versus unselfish. As a sales rep, most of the time you can be selfish and just be concerned about your customer. As a leader, you need to be concerned about others. You tell really good salespeople to worry about ten people they're responsible for? I've seen that disaster too many times."

"You saw it with me," Ryan agrees. "I carried my ego into my first leadership job, and I made everyone unhappy. We talk about happiness a lot, but how many leaders commit to changing course or know what they are doing is making their people unhappy?"

All the steps and stories in this book are about high performance and generating results, but they are first and foremost about becoming the person you want to be and creating the culture you want for the people around you. They are about looking inside yourself. They are about mastering what we used to dismissively label the soft skills. Those skills are really the hard ones—and today they are the most valuable.

Everybody has a great idea. Everybody has platforms, technology, data, systems, process, and customer relationship management. Not everybody has great relationships. Not everybody can express love to another person that they work with. Not everybody has a culture in which people love coming to work every day. Not everybody is open enough to realize the importance of this on an individual and organizational level—to hit that reset button to get even more performance and results from themselves and their people by leading through all these steps. But we all *can* be if we are willing to take a hard look at ourselves at every stage of our careers and start over.

No matter how successful we have been individually or how valuable a brand our organizations have become, we need to learn to evolve and find new ways to grow our businesses as we step into leadership—all while remaining profoundly human.

"Once I understood the importance of creating that kind of culture, I absolutely loved getting up and going to work every day, and I wanted the people around me to feel that way too," says Ryan. "When I first started managing, I pressed way too hard. Frank helped me see that. My boss, John, helped me see that. He was patient with me and became an incredible mentor and friend. He invested his time to help me learn to lead more effectively and fulfill my potential as a leader, but balanced that against the demands of a high-performance environment. He invited me to his home on Thanksgiving, but he wouldn't have hesitated to fire me for underperformance. I respected that. I understood we had a responsibility to others and the business that superseded our friendship. I finally got what it meant to say that the best leaders love people and that the people who work for those leaders will follow you anywhere and stay loyal—not because they have to but because they *want* to."

That's exactly what Chad wanted when he wound up in his first leadership position. He was working at the Detroit Pistons, and his boss fired the person running the inside sales team. He asked Chad if he knew anyone who would take the job, and Chad told him he would like to do it. But that was basically all he had—the desire. Somewhere in that discussion was Chad's boss asking me what Chad would do if he was in charge. Ryan hadn't sent Chad Frank's book yet. All he knew then was he never wanted his team to feel like he did when he started out. His thoughts turned to what got him there: the 30 Steps.

Leading with the 30 Steps

Chad realized that if the steps were essential for his success, they could be for the people who worked for him. So he became the teacher for his people that Ryan was for him. He made binders with the steps in them and developed a two-hour training in which they would go through each step, with Chad telling stories around them. At the end of the training, the binder became their playbook and self-assessment tool.

"I wanted them to hold themselves and the team accountable to the 30 Steps—to keep looking at them and using them to ask what they were doing well and what needed improvement," Chad says. Since that first team, Chad has hired hundreds of people and inherited many more. He still believes now what he learned with that first team when he presented the steps. "In about three months, he can tell where people are on a scale from zero to ten for performance. If they're not willing to do simple steps like self-education, I know they are pretty low and won't separate themselves from the pack."

Chad also realized something beyond individual performance. He had turned the 30 Steps into a culture document. With his team working to execute these steps, the vibe around the office changed. "We were all striving to do better. Pushing each other. Asking more questions, studying more, taking more time, asking for help, sharing experiences, stories, and opportunities. We gathered every Friday morning to listen to training material and discuss it. It was fun, dynamic. The steps produced a great culture without becoming cutthroat or compromising performance. Everyone knew if they didn't eventually perform, they would lose their jobs. Everyone competed to move up the leaderboard. But they supported each other, and I supported them. I stayed really close to them, encouraging anyone who was down and struggling, showing low-activity numbers. But even better, teammates did that for each other. They didn't let each other's bad days become the team's bad days. They knew you couldn't get out of a slump that way. They lifted each other up and went to the 30 Steps to find a way out of it. Maybe it was an extra call or a handwritten note or asking for a referral or that last call that could change your whole world."

This was exactly the kind of culture Ryan wanted for his team: an environment that enriched their lives and provided a great experience. "That motivates people to act and makes work meaningful to *them*,"

Ryan adds. "That gives people a sense of belonging. That makes them feel they are part of something larger than themselves. A culture like that has leaders who help their people grow and live better lives while nurturing their best performance. If they were not getting results, Chad didn't yell, 'Make one hundred more calls.' Instead, he used the steps in a way I never expected to reverse engineer the problem to find out why. As a result, Chad helped people become more than they thought they were capable of. Maximized their potential for themselves and the profitability of the enterprise."

And if they were mastering those steps and becoming so much better at their jobs that they wanted and deserved to move up in their careers, Chad was happy to help them.

"If you asked people about me, the term *career development* would come up very quickly. 'He invests in people and tries to advance their careers,'" adds Chad. "But I didn't do that just to be kind. It was a deal: You make the work important to you and excel, and I will look after you and help guide your career as you grow. If you know I care and have your best interests in mind as well as the company's, then you will give me what I need, and we probably don't have to talk about work ethic and performance all that much. I don't need to manage your results. I'm going to tell you how I think this job needs to be done, and you are going to own that and want to work really hard to do it that way because it's good for you. Then my job as a leader is to give you all the tools and resources you need to do it well: training, honest feedback, course correcting, coaching. If that happens, then results will happen. If the results aren't there and we're doing all these things, then there's either a whole other problem that's happening in the organization or maybe you are just not cut out for this job. Maybe you would be better in PR or marketing. But regardless, if you do everything I ask, no matter what, you know I have your back. That's a much better motivator than 'do one hundred sales calls or else!' That gets old fast and builds resentment instead of lifelong friendships and loyalty."

Those lifelong friendships and the loyalty Chad earned as he rose through the ranks into leadership at the NBA's Detroit Pistons, the NHL's Tampa Bay Lightning, and the Cavaliers again were exactly how Chad got on the Dallas Cowboys' radar. When Jerry Jones Jr. called Chad about a job at the Dallas Cowboys in 2007, Chad had no idea why the Cowboys were calling him. He hadn't applied for a job there and wasn't looking for one. Jerry told Chad they had been interviewing people for a position leading in their biggest project ever: building the greatest, most expensive stadium in the world. Several of the candidates the team had interviewed so far had worked for Chad, and his name kept coming up. So they decided to talk to Chad about joining them. Jerry said he would fly to Cleveland, and Chad couldn't say no. The idea of being involved in that was enticing enough to hear what the Jones family had to say. After Jerry liked what he heard and saw in Chad and in his office—engaged team members, a bookshelf that functioned like a library for sales managers and reps, motivational signs hung on the walls—he asked Chad to come to Dallas to meet his father and his brother Stephen.

Chad hadn't interviewed for a job in a long time when he was invited to Dallas and needed a way for the rest of the Jones family to quickly understand what he was all about. He chose two documents. One was his career "family tree"—all the people who had worked for him, many of whom were in key leadership roles around the sports industry and might already have been considered for the job. The other was the 30 Steps.

The 30 Steps Cowboys Up

Chad handed copies of each document to Jerry, Stephen, and Jerry Jr. and talked about each of them. He used the 30 Steps to share how a sales office under his leadership would look and feel. He explained how he had used them at every team he worked for as a foundation for creating the culture and how he runs things. He made it clear that to work at the Cowboys, he would need to do things the same way.

The Joneses responded positively. They were excited about the 30 Steps. They knew they needed a bigger, different, and more proactive sales process. Then they explained why. Chad's position and his team were critical hires. They would be responsible for a personal seat license campaign that was new and on a scale that had never been attempted anywhere before. Personal seat licenses had existed previously, but nobody had ever used financing of them as a method to drive more revenue. The revenue generated from these licenses would fund half of the new stadium's $1.2 billion price tag. Nothing of that scale had ever been attempted by the current Cowboys' sales team or *any* sales team.

"Having the weight of the world on me to deliver on an unheard-of level for this family and its great team?" Chad recalls. "I was excited to have that level of responsibility laid on me. I craved it, in fact. If I could deliver, it would be phenomenal for my career. I talked it through with Ryan and my family. Everyone agreed the opportunity was too good to pass up. We moved to Dallas."

What Chad didn't understand until he got into the job was just how risky the whole idea was—$600 million in personal seat licenses would be the most by far that had ever been generated in the history of the NFL (the previous record was $120 million). When the Philadelphia Eagles built their stadium, licenses on the fifty-yard line sold for $5,000 each just to secure the right to buy a season ticket. Now the Cowboys were going to charge $50,000 for that same seat, in addition to the increases to the ticket prices.

"How do we know the market will support that?" Chad asked Jerry Sr.

"Because that's what we need," he responded.

Chad kept asking questions: What if people started bailing? What if we charged too much and people couldn't afford it? What if the economy crashes and people who could afford it suddenly can't? Jerry's answer to every question was the same: we will sell our way through fear and any circumstance that arises—an unwavering entrepreneurial spirit.

Jerry Jones was not acting just on blind faith. He had done his research, believed there was a market, and had the stomach for risk. He understood it was a huge gamble that there was a market for those tickets. The team knew a certain number of the current Cowboys season-ticket holders were not going to be able to pay the prices at the new stadium. But Jerry had a plan that simultaneously increased his risk and opened up a much larger market for the seats: He allowed fans to finance them like homebuyers finance a home. Instead of writing a $200,000 check for four seat licenses, they could make a 10 percent down payment and take a loan for the rest. Only instead of a bank financing the loan and a layer of bank approvals, paperwork, and fees, Jerry Jones would finance it all, adding an annual payment and interest to the customer's season-ticket charge until the loan was paid off. Worst-case scenario, someone couldn't make the payment. If that happened, the Cowboys would take the seat license back and resell it.

The team knew there was going to be a backlash to their plan, both from those ticket holders and in the media. And they were right. "Once the media got wind of our license fees and ticket prices, there were all kinds of stories about how this would not work, the Cowboys were set up for failure, and the market would never support this," Chad says. "One reporter even staked out our sales center and counted the number of cars that pulled into our parking lot for presentations. He went on the news to report that only eight cars pulled into the sales center in four days."

The conclusion: *no one is buying season tickets*.

But Jerry Jones never wavered in his belief. People had called him crazy when he bought the Cowboys in 1989 for $140 million—the first time *any* sports franchise in the world had been purchased for more than $100 million. By the time Chad started in 2007, the Cowboys were worth $1.5 billion. Chad had never met someone so optimistic, risk-tolerant, and willing to go into the world of the unknown.

And Chad was put in a key position to execute it all. That was pretty cool . . . and scary. All he needed to do was get his team selling, and they were behind when he started. They had a little less than two years left on the clock, and everything Chad wanted to do should have started more than a year earlier under ideal circumstances. He felt an incredible sense of urgency and pressure.

The team Chad inherited, however, did not share his feelings.

* * *

Immediately after Chad started, he interviewed all twelve members of the Cowboys sales team. This was the same sales team that had been in place as the Cowboys had grown more than ten times in value since Jerry Jones bought the team, so Chad's expectations were perhaps a little higher than most places he had started. What he found in the ticket office was a culture and vibe similar to many successful sports teams across the country that sold out all or most of their games and had huge fan followings: Everyone selling mostly reactively to incoming calls on a general phone line. The Jones family was right: the kind of selling this team did well was completely different from the proactive processes the team needed to sell the new stadium.

When Chad asked each member of the team about their work and what they wanted for their careers—what's possible at the Cowboys and in sports and overall—most of them were content with doing what they were doing the way they were doing it.

The Cowboys needed that to change.

Chad started small. He told them that the work ahead required the day to start at 8:00 a.m. and end at 6:00 p.m., and everyone would wear a suit and tie. Then he turned to training. Since none of them were answering the phone by saying their name, he made them practice it. Within a week of implementing those few changes, the sales staff was completely against him. Then he introduced the 30 Steps as a framework for their success. They looked at Chad as if he were telling them to root for the New York Giants.

"I got it. They had no incentive to change until now," Chad recalls. "What they had done in the past worked well for a team that basically sold itself. That would not work for the results the sales team was now accountable for, and the attitudes of many of them didn't reflect the desire to make any change, let alone quickly. One of the top people even told me that what the Jones family was trying to do would never work."

After Chad interviewed everyone on the team, he went to dinner with Stephen and Jerry Jr. and told them he only wanted to keep three of the twelve people.

"What else do you need to do this?" Jerry Jr. asked after it all went down.

Chad hadn't gotten that far. He only knew the team needed many, *many* more people to succeed. Jerry Jr. got with Chad and his right hand at the time, Doug Dawson, for two days trying to figure it all out. They created a matrix and filled it with the sales numbers they needed, the days they had to reach them, and ballparked the closing rates. By their count, they needed thirty-six salespeople and an equal number of support staff. But not just any people—the best people. No BS. Sports industry, career-driven, ready to roll. People who got that if they succeed at the Cowboys, it would be the ultimate springboard into something much bigger in their careers. People willing to work sunup to sundown, weekends, nights . . . people willing to go *all in* to deliver on this project.

The Cowboys needed thirty-six of those killers, and those people would not come cheap. They would have to pay them well above the industry rate to relocate immediately to Dallas for a job that would only be guaranteed for this twenty-four-month sprint and massively heavy lift.

The Jones family said yes to all of it. "Whatever you need to make this happen. We have $600 million on the line."

Now, how to find these people? The Cowboys had never hired that many people at once—neither had Chad or anyone he knew.

* * *

Chad started by looking for experience at other NFL teams that had built stadiums, but that was unproductive, because no other team came close to the scale and scope of the Cowboys' project. It was clear the team needed a plan as different as the Jones family's approach to financing the stadium. They decided to host a weekend job fair at a local hotel. To attract people, they came up with a tagline: "Making History."

Attendance was beyond what was expected. Jerry fired up the crowd before they met everyone in group interviews the first day. That night, Chad's team posted a list in the hotel lobby of the people they wanted to see again in one-on-one interviews the next day. In those interviews, he reminded all of them this was an opportunity to be a part of something that was unique and what this could mean for them if they executed: a powerful springboard to future job growth.

"You can be a part of this and have phenomenal two-year selling experience," he said. "Put that on your résumé when we're done, and we will work just as hard as we did on the campaign for you to get your next great job coming out of this." People got it. They found most of the people they needed that weekend and all thirty-six soon after, as well as the support staff and three sales managers to supervise them and report to Chad.

From the interviews, the new team went right into a boot camp-like training, and the 30 Steps were one of the first documents in their handbooks. Everybody from that day on knew that they had to live them in selling the new stadium, premium seat licenses, and financing. They practiced their pitches with Chad and Doug demonstrating how: they went into a studio and pitched each other, played the recordings in front of the team, and then had them record their pitches and play them to the team. As the team got to work, that practice, the 30 Steps, and the rest of their training guided them and helped them get past their fear of customer reactions. One of Chad's greatest triumphs was hearing the team make the pitch and having customers say, "Wow, that's not nearly as bad as I heard."

But while Chad had a team ready to run through brick walls, he wasn't going to let them run through each other to get there. "We had a fast-paced environment with lots of leads coming in. We talked about activity levels and how we needed high levels of activity—calls, emails, appointments, etc. Through it all, we stayed true to our beliefs and created a culture we could take pride in and feel a part of while we lived up to the Cowboys' expectations. We were not going to have that cutthroat environment. We were not going to get to where we wanted to kill each other. Happy hours, awards, rewards, recognition—we were a 'family,' especially as we were spending more time with each other than our own families."

Chad also made sure the leadership team didn't hover over anyone's shoulders. They knew what their and our goals were. But the leaders wouldn't manage those goals. They trusted their teams to hold themselves accountable for their activity and results. They emphasized teamwork from the 30 Steps, and their teams were grateful. They responded by helping each other for no extra reward but the team's overall success, and about a year into it, their work was strong.

Then, in September 2008, the economy tanked. The team was halfway into their selling and had generated all this momentum and suddenly, nothing.

"I swear to God, we didn't make a sale for three months," Chad says. "Dallas may not have been the worst place to be after the crash, but the headlines made it seem like the country was going to be standing in breadlines soon. And we're calling people and asking if they want to spend two hundred thousand dollars on Cowboys tickets? We felt we had no choice. We stood down."

Jerry Jones was having none of that and set Chad straight. "You know what you're going to do? You're going to act like that doesn't exist. There can be no excuses. We are right in the middle of this." This is what he had meant by selling through fear and circumstance when Chad first took the job.

So they did. They rallied and challenged themselves in new ways. They cast wider nets and got creative. They went deep into the oil and gas business for leads. They got lists of people who flew on fractional jets and owned boats. The department was energized again. The Jones family noticed too.

"The Jones family was very invested in the sales team and had engaged us throughout the sales process," Chad recalls. "They let us know how impressed they were with our people and systems and how well run and organized our reports were. They came to the sales center and sat in on meetings with us, even got on calls when we asked or joined us in the closing room. They attended our biweekly get-togethers when we honored our top ten. One day Jerry came down and just started signing footballs and throwing them out to the team. We felt like we were part of the family, which only made us want to deliver more. As our outer market sales blitzes started and the team sold through the recession, our culture never wavered. Sure, there were times, despite all the energy, when I asked myself what I had gotten myself into. There were times where I thought I was going to preside over the worst sales failure in the history of sports. But the team delivered: six-hundred-million-plus in personal seat license revenue and more than three hundred suite lease agreements."

Of course, that could have been it right there. But the Jones family wanted to double down on the sales process Chad's team created. They wanted it to influence and impact more parts of the company and help build a bigger and better Cowboys Way.

Chad thought this was great. He had a team that wanted to stay—and so did he. As Chad promised, everyone had written their tickets to the next job, but they had had a blast working together. Two years of being tested in ways none of them had ever been tested, coming up with new approaches and ideas, and delivering their best. All the highs and lows, all the emotions, all with people who loved each other. It was the greatest sense of accomplishment one could have in business, and they didn't want it to end.

With all this knowledge and talent sitting around, there had to be *something* Chad, his team, and the Cowboys could leverage for themselves and the industry. They found the answer in Legends Hospitality Management.

* * *

As we noted in step 13 of the 30 Steps, Legends started as a concession company. It evolved to add a division that provided the industry with outsourced sales capabilities for tickets that took off after Chad's follow-up won the Rose Bowl business back. It took off when Chad approached the Cowboys about using Legends to outsource the team's sales capabilities, as well as its processes and culture. And they said, "Go for it."

Chad's team of twenty-plus started offering Legends' services nationwide and was transparent about everything. They were proud of what they achieved and how they achieved it, and wanted to sell that to other organizations in the NFL and beyond. They knew, much like the 30 Steps, there's a massive difference between having a playbook and knowing how to execute it. You need systems for hiring the right people and training them and a culture that supports them. "We didn't hide anything in our presentations," Chad recalls. "We showed exactly how Legends would fit into their businesses and develop a culture that would be customized and personalized for their objectives, sales targets, and customers." For example, when the Atlanta Falcons hired Legends to sell all the premium seat licenses and suites, you wouldn't know it was a Legends office. The colors were all the Falcons colors. The reps carried Falcons business cards and wore Falcons lapel pins.

Which brings us back to the story that started the book: the 30 Steps painted on the walls of the Atlanta Falcons offices. "I had nothing to do with it," Chad says, hence his surprised text to Ryan. "Mike Drake, who worked for me on the Cowboys' stadium and knew the 30 Steps, ran the Falcons' project for Legends and had designed the offices there. He decided to paint them on the wall in the team's colors because he thought they would be good reinforcement for his people every day."

Chad had nothing directly to do with the 30 Steps ending up on the Cowboys' wall either. That was Doug Dawson, Chad's right hand on the Cowboys' stadium project, who had become vice president of sales for the Cowboys ticket group. He saw the 30 Steps on the wall in Atlanta and said, "We have to have that!" Doug says the reps love seeing it in front of them every day, not just hidden in binders like they were with Chad.

Mike and Doug making the 30 Steps the writing on the wall was something Chad wished he had thought of but went beyond what he imagined, let alone Ryan, who had left his career in sales and was now working on helping people like Mike and Doug as leaders. And Chad was going to give Ryan the chance to show what he came up with to the Cowboys.

Starting Over

Eight years after we first read Frank Pacetta's *Don't Just Fire Them, Fire Them Up* and he became our hero, we got to meet him. Chad was working for the Cavaliers again as vice president of ticket sales and had developed a program that invited the local business community to hear and meet a guest speaker with the purchase of a ticket to the game.

"I'm going to try to get Frank for one of these things," he told Ryan.

"If you do, I'm coming."

Chad called back a couple of hours later.

"Dude, you're never going to believe it. *I talked to Frank.*"

"You talked to Frank?!"

"He's coming!"

Ryan flew in for the dinner and even bought a new suit: "I was all polished up in my new suit, and Frank was *right there*. And he was great. We told him that he changed our lives. He said, 'Yeah, yeah, yeah.' We sat in the front row with him at the game. We recounted his whole book to him. We were so nervous. He thought we were crazy the way we talked about his stories."

"I can't believe you guys. I wish my wife was here," he said.

At the time Ryan was on the path to having a legit shot at the CEO job of his company, but he told Frank he'd really like to be out there doing what he was doing.

Frank said, "You should. *Do it. Take the risk.*"

Ryan listened. He took that risk. He quit his job and became an entrepreneur, starting his research, consulting, and speaking business in January 2009.

Maybe because Ryan started his career in a recession, he figured the next recession would be the perfect time to leave his job as a chief sales and strategy officer and open his own business. No.

"It was the worst time to go into business. I made forty-three thousand dollars the first year," Ryan recalls. "Meanwhile, Chad's got the Cowboys job and is cementing his rise in the sports industry. I remember he wanted me to come down for a Cowboys game, and I said I didn't know if I could, because I was working hard getting my thing going."

Chad remembers exactly what he said that set Ryan off. "I said I knew you were in start-up mode and told you I'd cover your plane ticket." Chad smiles.

"And I told you, 'You say that once. You never say anything like that to me again. Don't ever, *ever* offer to pay for my plane ticket.' That was a moment that made me say, 'I'm going to make this work. There is no other way.'"

But there was a deeper truth behind Ryan's bravado. "I was very fragile. I was all in, but it was a difficult time for me. I was in uncharted territory. I had been working for someone else my entire career. Now I'm out there on my own in a recession. My runway was twelve to eighteen months to take off, but it bothered me how much more money was going out than coming in. People around me were skeptical. 'You're going to be a what? A speaker?' They would ask me what I did, and I didn't know how to answer the question anymore. I had no identity. I was more than a little bit lost. And Chad knew it. We spent hours talking about launching my own business versus staying the course or interviewing for a job at another company. Chad always believed in me. No matter what I said, he was positive and optimistic, while I was thinking I completely screwed myself."

"I knew it was so good that Ryan quit that job. This was going to be so much better. He could build something that he couldn't before, and I made sure he knew it." And Ryan did. After speaking with Chad, he knew what he had to do: start over—*again*. Just as he had when he first heard Jim Rohn speak. Just as Chad had after Ryan sent him the 30 Steps.

Eight years into Ryan's business in 2016, it wasn't Frank Pacetta who Chad hired to speak to the Cowboys about leadership. It was Ryan.

"It was the Cowboys' second annual executive retreat," Chad recalls. "The Jones family hosted at their ranch over two days, and it was the most formal thing we did with them. I was responsible for putting together the agenda: ten leaders presenting their business for about thirty minutes—a look to the past and a look to the future. We broke the business up with fun ranch activities, like fishing and skeet shooting. The second year, I decided to add a guest speaker on the first day to get us thinking about the whole culture of the organization, and I decided that speaker should be Ryan."

Ryan was psyched. He customized his presentation for the Cowboys and worked with Chad to come up with an agenda. It was all going great, until Chad started to get super anxious. "I felt there was so much pressure on him, and if it didn't go well, I was the one who screwed it up by choosing to bring my brother into the executive retreat. 'What the hell was that about?' they would say. I shouldn't have worried. Ryan killed it."

It was a full-circle moment for our brotherhood. We thought back to when we hated each other while sharing a room in high school. Now we were choosing to share a room at the Jones family ranch. That retreat was a seminal moment on our journey through sales, leadership, and building businesses. We didn't just think of each other differently; we *saw* each other differently. Ryan saw Chad in charge of this executive retreat and the respect that his employees had for his brother. Chad saw how much Ryan had seen and learned from speaking to and working with organizations nationwide and how much he could teach about leadership. What Ryan had seen was a massive gap between what organizations and their leaders said they valued versus what was being communicated and lived, articulating many of the things Chad had experienced in his career.

When Chad hired Ryan a second time to speak to the Cowboys' leadership team, Ryan had returned to his 30 Steps roots and created a new list to help leaders lead. He called it "11 Laws for Leadership." This time Chad was inspired to create something on his own, and when he agreed to do some speaking to people in his industry, he was inspired to develop his own list: "8 Principles for Leadership." As we wrote this book, we thought about making those lists the second part of this book. Of course, we could have just presented each of our lists for leadership success and been done with it. But that's not how we roll. We decided to use our lists as an opportunity to test our assumptions and start over by bringing those lists together, creating a collaborative list for new, aspiring, and established leaders as a complement to the 30 Steps. What happened next is where the book continues in part II.

MAKE WORK BETTER

"YOU'RE OLD SCHOOL, DUDE. You're suit and tie."

This was how Ryan thanked his brother for his birthday present? Chad had scored tickets to see U2 in Norman, Oklahoma. U2 is like our shared religion, and Chad got not only tickets but the Jones family to loan us the Cowboy bus to take us and a bunch of friends up to Norman from Dallas. This was U2's first concert anywhere in Oklahoma in twenty-six years, and you could feel the energy, anticipation, and excitement in the stadium. We screamed as Bono said the last time U2 was here they were "just a bar band." He thanked Norman for the "upgrade to the big venue, a few blocks down the street." A little rain didn't bother the audience or the band at all. We danced. We drank.

Flying high after a great show, we headed to a bar a few blocks down the street to keep the party going. That's where Ryan showed his gratitude to Chad.

It started innocently enough. Ryan talked about how when they first got into sales, everyone was in a suit and tie, and the culture was FILO—first in last out; get familiar with the light switch. In at 7:00 a.m. doing prep work and then making calls straight from 8:00 a.m.

to 6:00 p.m. Maybe lunch at your desk and a bathroom break. After 6:00 p.m., follow-up notes until 9:30 p.m.

"Today that's old-school shit, eight to six," Ryan said through his beer.

"I'm still an eight-to-six person," Chad admitted. "That's the minimum, I tell the team. You really want to be there at seven thirty and sending follow-ups."

That's when Ryan said, "What? You're old school, dude. You're suit and tie."

"You don't know what you're talking about anymore. Go back home and do some more speeches."

"You really think they are working those hours even if they're there? You don't think they're on social media? On their phones? You can't control hours anymore. You can't control them. You can expect results, but you can't expect that."

"You're drunk. You have no idea."

Thing is, Chad recalls, Ryan did know what he was talking about. Even as he reacted defensively, Chad started thinking, *Maybe Ryan was right*. Of course, there was no way he was going to tell Ryan he was thinking that.

Chad kept turning the conversation over in his head until he got to the office Monday morning. He asked his four most senior people to come into his office and asked them, "If there's one thing about what we do here that you think the sales team dislikes the most, what is it? What's the one thing that everyone would like to change around here?"

It was Doug Dawson, the guy who had been with Chad the longest and later the painter of the 30 Steps on the Cowboys wall, who immediately said, "Eight to six."

The others nodded in agreement.

"You know what? Eight to six just ended. It's over. Let's think about how we want to communicate this and then get the whole team together. We'll have the same expectations but let people work how they want to work. No more, 'Where were you?'"

The result: "It was a relief," Chad says. "Eight to six created anxiety, especially if you were late. I want to get people super fired up about coming to work. I didn't want people to live like I did." Chad understood then and there that what that means is going to change over time. "Technology changed the way we worked since I started leading people. Everyone had laptops and cell phones to get stuff done from anywhere. I needed to remind myself of that then, do some self-reflection, and not let my ego get in the way."

"Chad let them see how self-aware and willing he was to adapt by admitting he had been wrong in clinging to the past," says Ryan. "That's what we strive for in our relationship and all the relationships in our lives. Through highs and lows—no matter how much our egos flare up; no matter how hard we compete with, push, and challenge each other—we are open, honest, and vulnerable with each other when we need advice or get some barstool feedback."

That humility and self-awareness is needed from leaders and companies even more today. In the wake of offices opening back up following the global pandemic, the idea of eight to six seems antiquated. We both know that in most service and sales offices if you try to impose any set daily schedule, let alone mandate five days in the office, you will fail to attract top talent and keep the people you have. Office and home are as integrated as work and life for many employees. What people covet is the flexibility and the autonomy to decide for themselves how and where they are working. They are looking for balance in their lives, purpose in their work, and empathy from their bosses as much as, if not more than, competitive pay.

While this is a major disruption, it is more a rapid evolution from the eight-to-six mindset that Ryan confronted Chad about rather than a complete inversion of the past. After all, Ryan has been working and leading remote teams in distributed organizations his entire professional career—the advertising agency he started his career at had fifty-six regional offices across the country. Chad got a picture of the 30 Steps on the wall of the Legends office at San Diego State that was put there by people he has never met who are led by people he has never met. The difference today compared to before the pandemic is most of the people in the organization were in those offices. They're not anymore.

Simply put, place is just not a barrier to employment. The future of work is hybrid. We are going to be working from home and the office for the foreseeable future. Even Chad, who loves being in an office and longed for it during the pandemic, is thinking differently about when, why, and how he needs to be in the office and on the road. He plans on traveling less, knocking things out on video calls more than ever. When he does travel and he lands at noon from a business trip, he's not making the forty-minute drive to headquarters like he used to. He's going to the home office ten minutes away. He changed his relationship to work.

Chad sees this flexibility as a continuum from the end of eight to six, and what the Cowboys have done to codify this is no different than many companies. Eliminate the hard-and-fast rules about when, why, and how people come into the office. "We want people in the office, and we think people benefit from being in the office. But our only rule is get the work done," says Chad.

That said, we are firm believers that interacting with people in person is still important on every level, and some people may need the office because they cannot, for personal reasons, work from home. They find solace in an office. But no one needs to commute one to two-plus hours every day just to prove themselves. That isn't productive and never really was. Doing the exact same work in a building that you could have done at home is problematic. Being forced to come in and then just doing video meetings and sitting at your desk accessing the same work you could access from home can be demoralizing. Work should be a place where you experience the things you cannot do at home: the human-centered things that are essential for performance and mental health.

"Things we talk about in the 30 Steps like mentorship, teamwork, practicing, and the collaboration that drives innovation still need the human touch and can falter if all we do is work at home by ourselves. The answer is a hybrid model that works for the people and the company. You give people the flexibility they need to drive the business forward. If we're going to ask people to come somewhere, you must create an experience that makes going there relevant to the result you are trying to get," says Ryan, who cofounded a company during the pandemic that is completely distributed. But the entire team comes together in person at regular intervals to connect on big ideas, make big decisions, and reinforce their relationships.

Of course, all this can challenge people like us, who learned to lead when the office was king. We need to know more than ever that we don't know everything and keep adapting and adjusting our leadership styles. Regardless of how a company works, it makes things like retreats and off-site meetings even more significant and important.

There must be humanity and humility in everything we do. We are not perfect. We mess things up. We don't know all the answers. And we shouldn't pretend otherwise. We should simply commit to creating a better future together.

PART II

THE 9 TACTICS

CHAPTER 5

THE NEW WRITING
ON THE WALL

SITTING IN RYAN'S CONFERENCE ROOM in Minneapolis in the summer of 2019, our first attempt to match up our two leadership lists—Ryan's "11 Laws for Leadership" and Chad's "8 Principles for Leadership"—got off to a typical Estis brothers' start. We began by reviewing Ryan's list, and from the moment Chad asked Ryan to remind him what his first law was, our conversation went from collegial to challenging.

"My first law is 'Put People First—Performance and Profitability Will Follow.' It's about leading in the service of others. Leadership isn't a job; it's a responsibility."

"My one thing about that is it is very broad."

"I agree. I'm not sure if it is on the list."

"But it's your first one." Chad stares at Ryan incredulously and smiles. "Okay, putting people first is a good statement, but my view on something like that is it's very vague."

"I agree. It's vague when you hear it out of the context of my keynote. My laws are buckets that hold a lot of things."

Chad nods. "My principles are more 'do this, and you will get better.' What are you really telling the leader to do? When I think about people making the transition from a job in which they just need to think about themselves to a job in which you are supposed to take care of other people and take responsibility for their development, I want to get into the how. I don't know what the how is from what you said. It's more of an overriding philosophy."

"Correct," Ryan says. "It's not an action. It's a big operating principle. The most important law of leadership. I deliver these laws from the stage when I'm presenting a strategic vision. So that's why I have broad categories."

"Mine are mostly about spending time with people and getting to know them personally," Chad responds. "Asking questions about themselves, listening—those are a lot of things leaders don't do."

"I think I have all those things in these laws," Ryan notes. "My second one is 'Practice Transparency.' Transparency leads to trust. It's not enough to tell people what you're doing. Explain your rationale for decision-making. That's not the way we grew up in business. Today people have a higher expectation for transparency."

"Agree! That's on my list too. I think it is really important for people to understand the why, too, like you said. I want them invested in understanding the reasons things are happening. So we're good there. What's next on your list, then?"

"'Decide How You Show Up.' It's about the presence or disposition of the leader. It's doing things that put you in a position to be the best version of who you are when you walk into the door."

Chad pauses and then looks at Ryan. "Again, that all sounds very—"

"Vague?"

Chad, realizing he's now said this twice about Ryan's laws, tries to find a way forward: "I mean, we could build on it. I think we can have more of an impact by giving more of those action items. A lot of leaders want to get better but have no tactics around that. I think there's probably ten things that if a leader did well and were specific and they showed up and did well, they'd probably be damned good leaders. What's next for you?"

"'Conduct Little Experiments.'"

"What's that?"

"It's not being afraid to fail and how you manage around mistakes."

"Listen, I'm going to be a little challenging here . . ."

Ryan looks down. "Every time I started a book and whiteboarded it out in the morning, I would come back after lunch and say, 'This sucks. My brother won't give a shit about this.' You have to this time. You're writing it with me. But I'm beginning to understand why I never wrote a book with you before."

Recognizing our "discussion" of our lists was not going anywhere, we decided to take a different approach. We filled a whiteboard with Ryan's big-picture strategic laws of leadership and Chad's tactical principles and everything we talked about as we wrote them down, looking for connections and common ground. After a couple of hours, we had the new writing on the wall to make sense of, together (that's a photo of the actual whiteboard we filled at the start of this chapter).

Stepping back from what we wrote, we realized why it was so hard to combine our lists. Most leadership books are written from the perspective of a person or people who are either leaders within companies, teachers who study business and leadership, or leaders who have moved on from their leadership roles and became teachers. We had *two* of these kinds of people working on a book at the same time. Chad is a leader within a company. Ryan left the corporate world to become a teacher. To come up with a list that honored both our perspectives—the tactical practitioner (Chad) and the strategic teacher (Ryan)—was a bigger challenge than we imagined.

It took us months of testing and retesting our thinking against our ideas and our stories against that initial writing on the wall, but we finally settled on a list of nine tactics that have helped and *still* help us be better leaders. Together they represent our collaborative list of the essential things we feel leaders need to do to create a culture that people can't wait to get up and get to work in—and keep them "all in" once they get there. The first tactic ("Focus on *Their* Development") may have been based on Chad's first principle of leadership, but all the tactics are informed by Ryan's first law and their overriding philosophy: "Put People First—Performance and Profitability Will Follow."

We believe most leaders want to do that and make work better for their people. Yet most leaders, especially in sales, start their careers working in the same hierarchical, command-and-control cultures we did. If we told some of our first bosses to be transparent and explain the why behind what we were doing, they would have yelled, "Be transparent and explain the why? You want to know why? Because I told you to."

It's no wonder why "leaders" are the number-one reason, according to Ryan's research from dozens of companies, that only around 30 percent of people love coming to work. That number points to a real disconnect between leaders who say people are their priority and what they are doing to prioritize them. The 9 Tactics undo that disconnect by forcing leaders to stop managing around activity (results) and start prioritizing people to create an environment that has everyone wanting to do more, stretching to reach their full potential, and delivering big results in even the most demanding and difficult times.

We just had no idea how demanding and difficult those times were about to get.

* * *

On March 5, 2020, we finished the final draft of the nine tactics and the manuscript for this book and were outlining next steps. On March 11, 2020, the novel coronavirus disease COVID-19 was declared a pandemic by the World Health Organization, and the country began to shut down. Within weeks, Ryan saw his entire 2020 event calendar canceled or postponed, with no sense of when—or if—any of it would return. Chad flew home early from a long-awaited vacation with his family to close the Cowboys headquarters and set up his people remotely, wondering what the future held for them, the team, the NFL, and businesses that depend on them. Then, in May, Ryan watched from his balcony as his beloved city of Minneapolis fell into protest and chaos following the tragic death of George Floyd, followed by cities across our nation. And, of course, there was the presidential election stoking divisions between us.

Whoa.

It wasn't until March 2022 that we were able to move forward on this book again but asked if we needed to change our approach. We had started our book in one world and seemingly finished it in another. Ryan expected to spend weeks questioning and rewriting the content for a post-pandemic world, especially the 9 Tactics. Instead, he found himself nodding and thinking they were *more* important than ever.

The future of work is human, Ryan noted, and the 9 Tactics reinforced what the world of work needed moving forward—human-centered leadership—and helped answer an essential question: How do we make work better?

CHAPTER 6

9 TACTICS FOR BEING A MORE HUMAN-CENTERED LEADER

THE GLOBAL PANDEMIC and its Great Resignation, or Big Quit, with employees voluntarily resigning from jobs in unprecedented numbers and those who stayed demanding flexibility and a whole different level of support from their leaders and companies, has dramatically accelerated the need for those leaders to reflect on what it means to put people first in a post-COVID world. Yet few leaders have the self-awareness and soft skills necessary to make the transition to human-centered leadership. In fact, Gartner research showed only 47 percent of managers felt prepared to lead with empathy.[21] The 9 Tactics are all about having empathy for the people we lead in a world where the future of work is human.

Simply put, the world of work has changed, and leaders must change with it. Dramatic shifts from what people want to do to who they want to do it for to where and how they want to work have created a once-in-a-generation moment to reframe what work means in our lives and reimagine and redesign the way we lead. If you think we are going back to the way things were, then you have already lost. Everyone in the workplace, but especially millennials and Gen Z, are reconsidering how their leaders make them feel and their relationship to work. While we would have stayed unhappy in a job if it furthered our career, a 2022 study from Randstad found that more than 56 percent of millennials and Gen Z would rather be unemployed than unhappy at work.[22] This compels leaders to facilitate a new kind of relationship with them to not only help them maximize their potential at work but create fulfillment in their whole lives.

That's the opportunity and responsibility of leadership today: We want our people to be healthy, find purpose, feel a sense of belonging, and take control of their lives and careers; we just can't expect them to do it the way we did or on our terms anymore. Like many leaders today, when we started our careers, we oriented our lives around our work. That's shifting as generations behind ours reorient their relationship to work around their lives. They want control of their time. They desire fulfillment outside the workplace. They demand flexibility and balance. The 9 Tactics are your invitation to hit reset with more humanity and self-awareness. To develop the EQ and relationships that are necessary to lead people who want to feel valued by their companies and leaders, value what they are doing, and feel a connection to something larger themselves. Our 9 Tactics are a framework to help you prepare for the impact this will have on how you lead—to elevate your humility and confidence at the same time to engage people and invite people to give and get the best.

We all need that more than ever as we search for a sense of belonging and connection to others in what we do, feel what we do has meaning, know we are valued, and believe we are contributing to something special. We felt all these things during the pandemic. Even though we work in very different environments and have very different tolerances for how we work—Ryan does not want to work for anybody ever again and detests being told what to do; Chad thrives in his position between the Cowboys' leadership and the rest of the company—we both more than ever felt the need for belonging in ourselves and from the people who worked with and for us.

Ryan had an existential crisis of belonging during the pandemic. As every one of his speaking events and trips canceled in 2020, he asked himself: *I built this business as a thought leader the last twelve years and got pushed off the treadmill, so what do I want the next twelve years to look like? What is working and not working? Who am I becoming?* As he thought these questions through, he took the time to watch the magic of the sunrise to start the day with clarity, peace, and confidence, learned to cook, and made himself take walks along the local trails he never found the time to explore before. Soon, however, he realized what he missed was working with people.

That's when Ryan and three friendly competitors of his in the speaking world realized they could be better together and decided to merge their back offices and collaborate to form a new company. The pandemic had made all four of them realize they didn't want to do this work alone anymore. They wanted to feel a sense of connection and belonging to something larger than themselves. So they started sharing resources, developed best practices, and then launched a new company: ImpactEleven.

Culture, teamwork, and relationships have been critical to the way ImpactEleven has hired and framed what they are doing. Ryan could see the 9 Tactics manifested in the company's desire to make the world of work a better place by maximizing the impact they have on their employees and each other first, then their clients, and finally their shareholders and partners. He felt the tactics in the team's creation of a very clearly defined why (to put talented people with a powerful message in position to make an impact on the world); vision (to develop and serve thousands of voices with infinite influence, having a transformative impact on real organizations and real people's lives); and core beliefs (I got your back; we are trustworthy and authentic; we honor each other's work; we respect the collective; we operate with kindness).

While Ryan worked his way through his crisis to find belonging in a new company, Chad was longing for the office. Working from home, staring at a screen all day, having online meetings after online meetings did not energize him the same way being in person did. To get away from the screen, he had developed different habits, but they were mostly solitary: Hitting golf balls every day at 6:00 p.m., going on walks, riding the Peloton. It was a lonely time, and while he enjoyed the time home with his family, he missed seeing his work family in person. Chad loves his team, loves meeting in person and doing business dinners and trips. He wanted to be back in the mix because he finds belonging in the work he does at the office and being with the people who work with and for him. He wants to be there when they come in and need him. He had no interest in working from home once the lockdown ended, and the world started to go out again.

But as we said at the end of part I, Chad had already started to change his relationship to work before the pandemic when it came to flexibility, and that continued as the office opened again. He knew the team expected this too. So he does work from the home office when it maximizes his time with his family. He is trying to lead by example and not overbooking himself and go out four nights a week to find better balance between work and the time he takes for his family and all his relationships as well as the things he loves to do outside the office.

That said, flexibility like these tactics do not replace the need for hard work, and just because none of them say "results" doesn't mean they conflict with them. These tactics are *not* bottom-line averse and can be the catalyst for building great businesses. Taken together, they are a method for achieving the best performance from your people—inspiring and binding them together by making them, you, and the entire organization better through consistent and courageous communication, by creating alignment around shared goals, and elevating engagement. They are about stretching people to perform and maximize their potential while respecting their humanity and their different priorities, histories, and expectations.

If you need any proof of these tactics' ability to deliver better results, remember that Chad may have not articulated these tactics the way we have in the book when he started working for the Cowboys, but he had already been leading with them when he built his first team at the Cowboys. That team, with the full support of the Cowboys, delivered what the team needed to build what was in 2009 the most expensive stadium ever built in the United States—and is still top ten in the world—and then informed the culture of a new business: Legends Hospitality Management.

As a leader, you're inviting people to join you on a journey toward a compelling future state fraught with opportunity. That journey requires what Chad gave his team as they pursued the Cowboys' stadium project: A compelling vision of the future and a clearly articulated game plan for getting there. Results flow from the pursuit of that vision as they did for Chad. The stadium was a physical manifestation of the first step in the Jones family's vision for the Cowboys redefining what it meant to be a sports team and brand. That they were willing to take incredible risks to get there only inspired Chad more. "We were going to build that stadium and be a part of that vision. As a result,

I wanted to win for the Jones family even more than the company. I wanted to deliver for *them*."

That's a key word Chad just said: *deliver*. Like a promise, a vision is something you deliver on as a leader. Do you have that vision, and do your people want to deliver on it? Ask yourself:

- *What's your clear and compelling vision of the future?*
- *How are you communicating that to your team?*

Ryan first learned to ask and answer these questions from the best boss he ever had. "His energy, confidence, and optimism around our future success was contagious. We believed we would be a part of building it. That confidence and conviction earned our commitment. I would constantly leverage his vision as a source of inspiration for our sales organization. It made us resilient. As a result, we had the conviction and confidence to overcome challenges and difficulties."

Your being able to answer these questions gives people what they need so they can deliver on what you need. The effort you pour into them will create velocity in that direction. This is crucial because there is virtually no way to genuinely do the nine tactics on this list well if you're complacent about defining where you want to go. That's what we see as a big part of our jobs as leaders today—helping people understand that while they do not need to sacrifice for work the way we did in the past, they do need to invest in whatever they are doing and own it. In fact, from the first tactic, they require you to encourage and help people to decide what they want and invest in their careers—to decide what they want and then invest all they have and go for it.

The nine tactics help leaders inspire people to deliver outstanding performance while remaining profoundly human. All they require is shifting your mindset and doing the work.

PREPARE FOR IMPACT

Each tactic presents three keys to success when it comes to developing your skills around that tactic. Like the 30 Steps, each tactic ends with a series of questions. Take the time to think about and answer all of them. Then ask yourself: What's going to be different tomorrow for you? What decisions and commitments to your team can you make and actions can you take right now to be a more human-centered leader?

1. Focus on *Their* Development

Development of your people drives their commitment, accountability, and performance for you and the organization. If people feel you have their best interests in mind, then there's very little need for more motivation around performance and results. "What you get back are all the things you hope for as a leader," Ryan says. "Not only effort but loyalty, better decision-making, and the willingness to be a great teammate. What you get is buy-in, and the bottom line is that development is what people want."

KEYS TO SUCCESS
- Meet people where they are
- Coach
- Let go

Only 20% of employees say their leader always takes an active role in helping them develop their full potential.[23]

MEET PEOPLE WHERE THEY ARE

Chad's commitment to development starts in the recruiting and interview process: "When we built the team for the stadium project in Dallas, we made sure people knew before they walked in the door that if they did the right things, the right way for our team and the organization, there was no limit to where they could go. We wanted them to have high aspirations for their careers, because it went hand in hand with the expectations and commitment they will need for their jobs. Then we didn't have to talk about effort very much. When someone really believes that you are focusing on them and where they are going with no ulterior motives it doesn't take much to get that person to believe in what you are doing. They care about the company and results and want to put in the effort to deliver them."

But while career development may be first and foremost in many people's minds, careers are not the only focus. Work and life are highly integrated today. Thus, professional and personal development are too. What does the big picture look like to them? What do they want their days to look like? Their lifestyle? What kind of people do they enjoy being around? What do they love to do? Where do they want to live? Where do they want to be in five years to support all those questions and their careers?

Some people will say "I don't know" when asked those questions, and that's okay. Start seeing if you can help them think about *some* vision for their future even if that means multiple careers. Even if someone says, "I just want to have as much money as I possibly can," it at least helps you help that person plan toward something—*anything*. After all, if they aren't clear with their own development, they are likely less clear on what they want from their job with you.

"If you can't express what you want your future to look like, it's hard for me to help," says Chad, "I meet a lot of young people starting their careers who have not yet decided their careers are that important to them. If they continue that route, that's a recipe for getting stuck. I can meet you where you are and help you sort through things, but I can't make where you're going important. You control your future. If I know what you want, I can help you get there. That has nothing to do with the company or me. It's 100 percent about the person sitting across from me. It's about where they're going when they deliver the performance we expect. You're ultimately the CEO of your future and career, and I'm here to help you manage it. For me, it is always about treating people the way I would've wanted to be treated if I was in their jobs. I was grateful when people treated me this way, and people are grateful when I meet them where they are and make them think about where they're going."

What if someone doesn't care about advancing their career and says, "I'm happy being an account executive?" It doesn't mean they don't know or don't care. It could mean they are not interested in movement or mobility. People who aren't looking for upward mobility can still grow within their current role and get better at it. Chad is happy to know that about people who work for him and for them: They've recognized that not everybody is cut out to be a leader. But Chad then tells them they still must keep learning. They must keep doing the 30 Steps. But if they're good with that and have a great attitude because they have decided they are where they want to be, then his job is to help them settle right in and stay engaged.

COACH

Understanding where your people want to go is only the start of the development conversation, because people's needs often change over time. People willing to run up every hill and get three promotions by the time they're twenty-eight may not want the same thing at thirty-five or may want *more*. People killing it in sales may be ready to make the jump to leadership or be happy killing it where they are. People willing to stay late and be a weekend warrior could feel differently once they have a kid. Development means committing to getting them where they want to go, whether that goal is to have a family or be a vice president. Or both.

The only way to know if priorities have shifted is to *keep* meeting people where they are by coaching them through, up, and even out to help them meet their and the company's goals. The difference between managing and coaching is the same as it is in sports. Managing is about organizing and developing the teams and processes to put the best team "on the floor." Coaching is about helping people reach their full potential once they are on the team and in the game by personally investing and developing them, caring about who they are, and driving the best performance out of that team together and as individuals.

Think of it this way: Ryan didn't manage Chad through the 30 Steps; he coached him. He didn't expect the steps to do the work for him. They were a framework for success, but Ryan's investing time with Chad was as important as Chad investing time in the steps.

Ryan defines *coaching* as asking not telling, listening not talking, and helping people take responsibility for accomplishing what they want to accomplish. This investment of time and energy must be constant. "This is what differentiates Chad as a leader," says Ryan. "People would call him their coach, not their boss. And not just a coach in work but in life. People are in his office talking about the personal, not just the professional because work and life are integrated. He is coaching people through it all not just as a boss but as a guide, tactician, friend, mentor, and expert. And he's doing it all with the best interest of the people across from him in mind. He knows if they win, the Cowboys win, so helping people get clarity on where they want to be in life and getting buy-in around that is just the first step. He works with them to get there using the next tactic. He knows coaching them through the present is a condition of getting them where they want to go, because you have velocity and momentum now to go where you want to go."

This approach to coaching didn't change when Chad became a leader of leaders. The shift only reaffirmed just how hard it is to have the coaching mindset. When he pushed his coaching expectation down to his direct reports and less experienced leaders, many struggled to follow his example. So Chad coached them up on how to execute his philosophies and their importance to their future, not just the people they lead.

Many leaders, consciously or unconsciously, think and worry about themselves first. They hold their kick-ass people back to protect their area of responsibility. They don't want to spend time talking to people and developing their careers even within the company, promoting them up or to another department or even out to another organization. All that means is they have to replace them. What Chad wanted his leaders to realize is that mindset not only holds their team's growth back but also might be holding *their* growth back. Remember: The Cowboys might never have found Chad if he hadn't put so many leaders out into the world. Those people also created a referral network for the future talent he needed.

Instead of focusing on your success and just managing the team's success, focus on how you can be a coach and help them take ownership. It isn't easy, but it's the right thing to do. Create opportunities to help people contribute more to the business. Invest in helping them achieve their full potential—and let them do it. Eliminate barriers that might inhibit success.

LET GO

Giving up things you don't need to be doing like running meetings or making sales calls can be about insecurity ("No one will do it like me"), ego ("I want the credit"), and/or fear ("I need to show work product, or I'm going to get fired"). Those things are the major killers of culture and success with the tactics on this list. But failure to let go is not always about objectively negative actions. It's natural to want to hold on instead of letting go. It's comfortable, and the more important the situation and bigger the deal, the harder it is to face that discomfort. Even a leader as self-aware as Chad who empowers his people to act autonomously still finds it uncomfortable to let go.

"I had two people on my team preparing to lead a presentation," Chad recalls. "When they showed it to me, I wasn't presenting any of the slides. I like doing that. I kept thinking, *Am I really going to let go of that? I'm just gonna sit here while these two people do the presentation?* Part of me never loved it, but it was the right thing to do. It was their job. They trusted me to let them, and I trusted them to do it. That was a real evolution for me and key to their development."

Even after this teachable moment, Chad still had to work at this part of the tactic to prevent himself from stepping in. "When I first told my right hand I wasn't going to run a sales meeting—that he should be running it—I stopped going. If you told me a couple of years before that I wasn't going to sit in the sales meeting, I would've said, 'No way, that's my thing.' Now I'm no longer in most sales meetings unless I'm invited. I let the organization see that, and it gives him confidence and the team confidence in him."

That's putting people first when it comes to development, and the more you do, the more you get in return, including time, which you'll need for the next step.

PREPARE FOR IMPACT:
FOCUS ON *THEIR* DEVELOPMENT

KEYS TO SUCCESS

- Meet people where they are.
- Coach.
- Let go.

ASK

- Do you know what's most important to your people?
- How often are you having future-directed conversations with them?
- How are you coaching your people to empower them to get where they need to go?
- What responsibilities are you holding on to that you could let go of?

2. Go for Coffee

Most businesses are set up to have people focus on things *other than people*. Put your phone down, close your laptop, and give people not only your time but your undivided attention. The way we show up and how present we are when we do matters. In the end, if you don't care enough to focus on people and put them first, then you will fail no matter how much time you make. All this is why when Chad speaks at industry conferences, the slide that says "Go for Coffee" resonates deeply. Leaders always come up to

> Two-thirds of employees believe management does not care about them on a personal level.[24]

him to say how much they love the idea and need to get better at it. It's easy to understand the appeal. Chad calls these coffees "catch-ups," and they can cover anything as long as there is no hard agenda. Agendas are for more formal meetings, reviews, and training sessions, whether inside an office or virtually. Those meetings can be fun and conversational, but they have structure and focus on a specific purpose. Going for coffee is really a metaphor for the most human side of personal development and relationship building, which is why in the age of remote and distributed teams the "going" can also be virtual. It's about making the time and holding the space to create a genuine conversation with your people away from formality and toward seeing the whole person who works for you, which deepens engagement and relationships, especially if people are still operating remotely all or part of the time.

KEYS TO SUCCESS

- Ask, "How are you doing?"
- Be present and listen.
- Make time and hold space.

ASK, "HOW ARE YOU DOING?"

When Chad told Ryan going for coffee should have no hard agenda, Ryan argued it should at least have an objective. The second Ryan spoke, he knew what Chad was going to say. "Don't hijack my coffee meeting with your BS form from HR." Ryan then proposed at least preparing questions in advance. Chad again resisted. He didn't think that was wrong—just that it would make people like him nuts.

We're both right.

For a leader like Chad, who has created a culture that puts people first; focuses on development; and knows how to ask open-ended who, how, why, what, and when questions from the 30 Steps, the art of the coffee conversation is easy to master. But tell less-practiced leaders to go for coffee and that might not go so well—and yield zero benefit for the time spent. In fact, it might make things worse.

Too many leaders (and people in general) treat "conversations" as a one-way street. They talk *at* people, failing to ask a single question, or even worse, they talk the entire time, making the conversation about them, not the person sitting across from them. That's why Ryan argued leaders need to be thoughtful about objectives. "It would hurt Chad's brain if every time he went for coffee he had to write down his objectives and map out the questions he wanted to ask. But there was a time when even he didn't do it so well. He's just done it for so long that it has become a habit."

To be clear, not going to coffee and having these conversations with your people doesn't mean you can't be a good leader. But it changes the relationships you have with your people—and that affects the overall culture.

"I worked for someone for four years who never asked me one question about myself ever," Chad recalls. "We never went for coffee, a drink, or a nonworking dinner. We didn't develop a relationship. We were just working together. That doesn't lend itself to anything beyond doing the business and talking about performance. That's missing the personal connection."

We both want that personal connection with the people who work with us. Our advice if you're just starting the coffee conversation is don't think too much. Sit down and say, "How are you doing?" That can be your objective—to find out how they are doing on a personal, not just professional level. That moves naturally to how things are going, how they are feeling, what's going on in their lives, and anything else they'd like to talk about—and then listen to the answers.

BE PRESENT AND LISTEN

Asking questions is an essential skill, but active, perceptive, deep listening that focuses on others and leads to thoughtful follow-up questions demonstrates results in genuine communication and is the foundation of any relationship. Ryan calls this "relational competency—being present with presence": Put in the work to listen and your people will feel you care for them as much as your expectations for results. Get people comfortable and they're really going to tell you how they feel about what's going on in their lives, their frustrations, what they're doing, and about their future desires. When that happens, we learn not only about who our people are but also about what is going on in our businesses that we might not see from inside the office.

"Those conversations can cover a lot of ground in giving and getting feedback and discovering how things are going, what people are focused on, and what they are worried or concerned about," Chad says. "They already know that I care about their development. We have a culture in which they feel very comfortable with me. That creates a level of trust. Going for coffee deepens that engagement, and we all know what happens when employees are engaged."

MAKE TIME AND HOLD SPACE

Most weeks Chad has at least three to five coffees—and not just with his direct reports. He makes himself available to everybody. If someone wants to have coffee, they just email him and he will make time, which is the biggest reason it doesn't happen for most leaders.

Chad is as busy as any leader Ryan has ever met, so where does he find the time for coffees that other leaders don't? Part of it is he practiced the first tactic and let go of things his team could handle. He cut down on unnecessary group meetings like "Monday-morning huddles" with direct reports and asked them to update him directly, which his direct reports appreciated greatly. He also gets in early. But those are tactics, none of which he could execute successfully if he didn't have the mindset that spending time with his people is one of the single most important parts of his job.

"Too many leaders feel they are not working when they spend so much time with their people, in and out of the office, formally and informally," Chad says. "I'll have a day when I have coffee with someone in the morning, then have a couple of one-on-ones, have two people come into my office to work out a problem with me in the room, attend three meetings, and finally get a drink with of my reps for ninety minutes to talk about anything and everything before I go home. Too many leaders would look back on that day and think, 'I wasn't productive. I should be doing my job.' No, that *is* your job."

In fact, plenty of the leaders Ryan has worked with have used the "I'm too busy doing my job" line as an excuse for why they can't spend more time with their people. So did he when he started his leadership career. "Big miss," he says. Chad's mindset that it *is* the job eliminates that excuse. You just need to organize yourself in a way so you can do it. Maybe not 100 percent of the time, but at least 25 to 30 percent.

Here's how Ryan approaches organizing time in his executive coaching:

- Ask what's most important to them (every leader will say some version of "our people").
- Audit their calendar and how they schedule their days and spend their time.
- Map that time out and see how much they spend aligned to their priorities—that is, people.

"What you realize really quickly is that most leaders' schedules are out of whack," says Ryan. "They aren't spending 10 percent of their time with their people. They are overscheduled, overwhelmed, and exhausted by going to meetings they don't need to attend, holding meetings they don't need to have and poorly managing the ones they lead. They waste a lot of time micromanaging and not delegating. Why? Pressure to hit numbers, insecurities, demands from shareholders to grow. The 'shareholder first' mentality is starting to shift, but there's a long way to go to unlearn that. Chad wants people to feel comfortable talking about their fears and dreams so he can support them completely, but most leaders aren't spending as much time as he is with his people. If you're a leader as present as he is in your teams and organization, you're naturally having multiple collisions and one-on-one conversations every week. You get a lot of how things are going for people through those touch points."

Of course, what gets scheduled gets done, and too many leaders fail to schedule enough one-on-one time outside formal reviews. Even the most evolved leaders can get distracted and pulled in multiple directions. Combine that with the fact that in the age of hybrid work, there are fewer opportunities for informal and spontaneous conversations that get people to open up. Making time and holding space ensures that everyone has the opportunity for informal, future-directed conversations with you regularly.

GO FOR COFFEE

KEYS TO SUCCESS

- Ask, "How are you doing?"
- Be present and listen.
- Make time and hold space.

ASK

- How do you consistently support your people and their hopes, dreams, goals, and visions?
- When was the last time you had an informal conversation with them with no hard agenda?
- How much time do you schedule with your people?

3. Practice Transparency

Transparency leads to trust, and in the absence of trust you can't build a healthy culture or organization. There's also a direct relationship between the agility and resilience of a team and the transparency of its decision-making processes. It's not enough to tell people

57% of employees have little to no trust in their leadership.[25]

what you're doing. Explain your rationale for decision-making. And then make sure your expectations for the team to execute them are clearly defined.

> **KEYS TO SUCCESS**
> - Tell them the why.
> - Tell the truth.
> - Define expectations.

TELL THEM THE WHY

When the Jones family decides on a new initiative or course of action for the Cowboys or makes an adjustment, Chad asks questions to understand the why behind the what, where, when, and how. Then Chad does what he did before he joined the team: he turns around and tells the team responsible for executing those things all he knows to make sure they understand the why as well as everything else. "I try to put them in the room. I want them invested in understanding the reasons things are happening. Why we are selling this product before another one. Why we are changing course on an initiative. Why we decided to go in this direction. I let them ask questions just like I did. If everybody understands the big picture around what we're doing and how they fit in, then there is a much bigger chance of them owning the work and staying bought in."

Chad knows that people today value information and have a higher expectation for transparency. The more transparency, the more trust. According to the Edelman Trust Management framework, companies know "ethical drivers such as integrity, dependability, and purpose drive

76 percent of the trust capital of business, while competence accounts for only 24 percent." Yet many leaders learned to do business the exact opposite way: Tell people only what they need to know. As a result, most organizations are operating with a trust deficit based on a faulty assumption. They think people will betray their trust—for example, sharing what they know to a competitor or the media—instead of realizing they're demonstrating and creating more trust by being completely transparent and doing the right thing.

Does that mean your trust won't backfire? Of course not. We must be comfortable with a little bit of risk with transparency. That isn't easy to accept, but it is much better than assuming your people already intend to betray you.

TELL THE TRUTH

Early in his leadership career, Chad had three internal candidates for a senior position, and he knew the ones he didn't pick would be really pissed if he didn't choose them. Few, if any, leaders look forward to those moments. No matter how many times we go through them, they suck. We know we need to be brutally honest about our decisions, but instead we make something up to soften the blow or avoid a blowup. That can make a bad situation even worse. That's why Chad decided to tell the candidates straight up what was going on. No made-up story, nothing designed to make them feel better. He simply said he picked the person he thought would do the best job and why.

"As expected, the reactions of the two I didn't choose were pretty harsh," Chad recalls. "One of them said it was unfair. One of them said I didn't understand the value of his experience. I let them vent and then ended the conversation by saying, 'I'm comfortable with my decision. I knew you wouldn't like it. And you might decide to leave because of it. So I'm gonna let you think about that, and you either have to come back and tell me that you're on board or not. If you want to look for another job, then I will help you.'"

One candidate left. The other came back a few days later and said he was on board. He did a terrific job. Years later he came into Chad's office and said, "I don't know if I have ever told you this, but you absolutely made the best decision. The guy you chose is a rock star." How cool is that? It's a perfect example of learning to say exactly what was going on and dealing with the consequences. It's the perfect example of how whatever pain that results in the short term from telling the whole truth and not lying not only goes away in the long term but can benefit you, your people, and the organization. Immediately addressing any issue quickly, openly, and honestly gets a way better result than allowing these things to fester. Understanding this will serve you well when you need the courage and confidence to attack the tactics of having tough conversations and being decisive. For now, consider what it means to the defining expectations of your people.

DEFINE EXPECTATIONS

We often talk about transparency as it is linked to decision-making and the transactional sides of business, less about expectations and role clarity. A shared vision has everyone working toward a common goal. Defining expectations, not simply setting them—communicating everything they will be accountable for in trying to reach that goal is essential. But those expectations can shift short and long term. Job descriptions can't accommodate this, which is part of the reason.

Instead of falling back on out-dated and static job descriptions, leaders should have accountability around a set of outcomes with clearly defined expectations and the roles your people will play to achieve them and why. Then be specific about what people can expect from you. As those outcomes and expectations are met (or unmet), create new and more evolved ones.

Research shows upward of 60% of job descriptions don't define the day-to-day reality of someone's role.[26]

The best bosses we have ever had were candid, clear, and consistent in communicating their expectations for performance. Their clarity meant we always knew exactly what was expected of us. The 30 Steps are an example of a clearly defined set of expectations for you and your team that communicate *how* to execute the right way to achieve any expected outcome—expectations that generate results without ever even saying the word. Top performers love this. They love being held accountable to these expectations and seeing their leader model that behavior and creating a culture of accountability.

PRACTICE TRANSPARENCY

KEYS TO SUCCESS
- Tell them the why.
- Tell the truth.
- Define expectations.

ASK
- Are you telling your people everything you can to understand the why behind the work they're doing?
- Are they operating with clearly defined expectations?
- How are you holding people accountable, including yourself?

4. Create Safety

Most leaders say they want their people to take intelligent risks, but when the risks don't lead to reward, results fall short of expectations, and mistakes are made, those leaders reveal how little they understand that all risks have consequences—positive and negative. Your people will never be incentivized to go big and do more in a culture that judges for their mistakes or methods. Do you want those people to work in fear and avoidance, doing the bare minimum and playing safe like so many others who are? No, you want to empower and encourage them to be bold. But without safety around risk, they'll play it safe out of fear of judgment—or worse.

The term *psychological safety* was coined by Harvard Business School professor Amy Edmondson. She defines it as "a shared belief that the team is safe for interpersonal risk-taking." Establishing a climate of psychological safety allows space for people to speak up, share their ideas, be vulnerable, and take intelligent risks. It's crucial to prioritize high psychological safety to create a high-performing team. People need and want to feel safe in their work relationships without disrespecting or denying the opinion of others or the culture of the team or orga-

> Only 17% of professionals believe trying new and untested ideas would be rewarded or approved by their supervisors.[27]

nization. Leaders must see the benefit of being inclusive to cultivate safety and generate growth. That requires more than trust. It requires an environment in which people are empowered and encouraged to take risks, even when mistakes and failure are inevitable. Create an environment that is safe for risk-taking and inclusive of differing opinions and methods, and they'll want to do more. They'll stay all in.

KEYS TO SUCCESS
- Encourage intelligent risk-taking.
- Be consistent.
- Know ego and insecurity kill.

ENCOURAGE INTELLIGENT RISK-TAKING

The Dallas Cowboys have a twenty-person media department that reports to Chad and operates like an in-house ESPN. It covers everything the team does, including the annual NFL Draft. One year the media team asked to go inside the Cowboys' "war room" to show how the draft-day business and strategy was done. They took pictures and videos and posted them in real time on social media. Everything was fine, until one of the pictures captured the number on the phone that sat in front of Jerry Jones—the number that the Cowboys used to get the most up-to-date information and to make deals with other teams.

Suddenly that phone started ringing with fans telling Jerry Jones what he should do ("Draft so-and-so, Jerry!") and what they thought of his picks ("Screw you, Jerry, for picking that person!").

"Holy, holy hell," Chad remembers thinking. "We went into 911 mode. We had to change our number on the fly. On one of the biggest days of the year. It was chaos."

The leader who runs the media department for Chad was devastated. It was a tragedy to him, and he expected a harsh reaction, from having the group's access to the team restricted to needing to fire the photographer who posted the picture to *him* getting fired. He got the exact opposite.

Chad explained that the situation wasn't great, but it wasn't tragic—just an honest mistake. He recommended his leader send the Jones family a note saying how badly he felt, that he was aware how much it had screwed things up, and promising to be a lot more cautious and careful in the future. "That's all you can really do," Chad said.

That's what the media department leader did, and Stephen Jones immediately responded and told him that he and the team shouldn't let up for one second. "This is exactly what makes us who we are. We can't be afraid to make mistakes. I don't want you to pull back one inch. We are going to keep going and doing things that others don't do. Appreciate the note. Let's roll."

"I saved that email for a long time," Chad recalls. "This leader had beaten himself up plenty. What would have happened if the Cowboys beat him up more?"

"He never would have taken a big risk again," says Ryan. "How you manage when a mistake happens is how you feel about safety. Is it an opportunity for learning and moving forward, or is it an opportunity to extract a pound of flesh? The media department leader probably will never forget that email from Stephen Jones. He'll never forget how safe and valued it made him feel."

"I'm anxious enough when I make mistakes, and some of those mistakes can involve numbers with a lot of zeroes. That keeps me up at night," says Chad. "If the Jones family isn't happy about them, it can get intense. But unlike other bosses I've had, I never feel that my job or the jobs of anyone who works for me are on the line because we went after something different or big, and it didn't work out. We feel safe because, in the end, Jerry Jones and the entire Jones family not only respect the effort but are comfortable with it. We all strive to live by something Jerry says all the time: 'I have never had a problem dealing in areas of ambiguity. I can make a decision and not have it all lined up just right.'"

Will I be judged for what I am doing if it is not the way the company has done it previously? Can I take intelligent risks? If your people are asking these questions, that anxiety extends well beyond mistakes to inclusivity and ensuring your people that their opinions are valid. It can lead to active disengagement. So many people are afraid to make mistakes at work that they are working to *not* get noticed—to not get fired. This lack of engagement is a less discussed part of what fuels "quiet quitting," in which employees do the minimum amount of work to not get fired and/or set boundaries to orient work around their lives. A 2022 Gallup poll showed that only 32 percent of employees reported being engaged at work.[28]

You can talk all you want about creating an environment that encourages people to keep pushing the envelope, but the truth is, if you're not making mistakes, you're not embracing innovation and generating engagement. It's not that mistakes don't have consequences, and if those mistakes keep costing you, heads might roll. But the safer you feel getting outside your comfort zone to take those risks, the more upside there is.

"Part of being a good leader is being comfortable being uncomfortable," says Ryan. "Our brains are wired to keep us safe, so we invent stories that rationalize the need for safety. Those stories replace the trust with a lot of fear and paranoia about something that might happen, and your people notice."

BE CONSISTENT

Chad once worked for an extremely successful entrepreneur who had collected all his approaches to leadership, his wisdom, and what he valued into a book he shared with his team. Chad loved it. The leadership philosophy on those pages was one he wanted to follow and still remembers to this day. Chad also remembers that after a few months on the job, he realized that his boss failed to follow the leadership philosophy he wrote about. He didn't live what he said he valued.

"I was totally turned off," Chad recalls. "I didn't have the courage at the time, but I would've loved to challenge him and say, 'That's a contradiction. You can't be the guy who stands up and writes a book and does the things you are doing.'"

We couldn't write this book if we did not live the 30 Steps. We couldn't write these principles of leadership if we didn't live them. Well, we *could* but everyone would call us out and we'd be just as hypocritical as Chad's old boss.

"That kind of inconsistency creates the kind of anxiety you try to avoid in everything you do as a leader," says Ryan. "It's hard to create alignment and make decisions. It's hard to course correct when you don't have these core foundational things and live them. Too many leaders in too many businesses run in the absence of these things. Or they don't mean anything."

Simply put, the 30 Steps on the Cowboys wall mean something because they are lived by the leaders who reinforce them with their actions. The words in that book Chad's boss handed out had the opposite effect on him and the culture of the organization. To be clear, Chad's boss had made a lot of money building his businesses. But if that's all you value—if that's the measurement of your success as a leader—then why not just say so? Be honest and consistent about what you value most, and you'll attract exactly the people you need to help you get there.

Part of what makes Chad and his team feel safe is the consistency in the approach that the Jones family showed from the top down. If mistakes are okay one week and the next week people get ripped apart for them, no one knows how a leader will react. That makes people anxious to take risks or push their limits because they're afraid to get it wrong. Chad also leads by that example. People know who he is and how he acts. He might be intense and emotional, wearing his passion on his sleeve. When something goes wrong, he might swear (a lot), but he's going to quickly come back to center and deal with it directly like he did with the draft-room screwup. "

That consistency lets them know he's got their backs, Ryan says. "That allows them to be themselves, own their mistakes, and even laugh about them later."

KNOW EGO AND INSECURITY KILL

A team member of one of Chad's direct reports asked to speak to Chad one day and scheduled a meeting. Chad thought nothing of it. He feels anyone should feel free to talk to anyone they want. He doesn't see any weirdness in that or worry about what his team is going to say about him. Chad's direct report saw things differently. He demanded his team member tell him what the meeting was about and that it should never happen with his knowledge again. All conversations would go through him. "Don't ever send Chad an email without copying me," the direct report told his team member, who told Chad. That's leading by fear, which is all about a leader's insecurities and ego.

Fear can be channeled by you into new emotions, positive thinking, and action like Ryan did after he saw Jim Rohn and jump-started his career. But fear isn't sustainable as a driver and can be a huge inhibitor when you're responsible for others.

"When I was first promoted into leadership, I said things like: 'Your number is now my number. We are not missing this number. And if we do, one of us is not going to be here next year. And I'm pretty sure I'm going to be here next year.'" Ryan remembers. "That was all my ego and insecurity talking. I projected my fear that something bad was going to happen to them, just like Chad's direct report did. Who wants to work for someone like that in the long run? All it does is make people anxious."

When you feel safe and valued like in any relationship, the answer to those questions and many more like them is yes. You are comfortable expressing your truths, not self-censorship or saying what you think somebody wants you to hear. That's what happened when Chad joined the Cowboys. He went into a high-performing organization and the most valuable and best brand in sports and challenged them. What he learned is that the best organizations want to get better. They have an appetite for improvement and a willingness to listen.

A secure leader will always stand up for what they believe but is also willing to challenge assumptions and take intelligent risks that lead to growth. An insecure leader holds onto the status quo with a death grip because they are afraid. That's the difference: Secure leaders have the confidence to let their people weigh in, challenge the status quo, find what works for them, and take intelligent risks on behalf of the organization.

PREPARE FOR IMPACT:
CREATE SAFETY

KEYS TO SUCCESS
- Encourage intelligent risk-taking.
- Be consistent.
- Know ego and insecurity kill.

ASK
- How do you empower intelligent risk-taking and manage through the mistakes that happen when you take risks?
- How do you avoid getting in the way of supporting your people's opinions and ideas?
- How do you cultivate psychological safety?

5. Build a Team Environment

Your responsibility is to find a way for everyone to have success, collaborate, and be happy for the successes of the people around them to work together and across the organization to drive results. A high-performance organization does not have to pit everybody against each other. Reinforce the positive behavior of the team and everyone individually.

People who view themselves as part of a team persisted 48–64% longer on a challenging task.[29]

KEYS TO SUCCESS
- Focus on fit.
- Celebrate progress (not just outcomes).
- Tear down silos.

FOCUS ON FIT

Leaders today need to have a talent-hunting mindset and be obsessed about finding, recruiting, and hiring great people. In fact, finding and recruiting talent should make up a portion of leaders' time even when they aren't hiring. That said, hiring the wrong people and holding on to them too long are two of the biggest costs any organization faces, and even the best leaders fail at this, especially the first part. That's clear every time Ryan asks leaders, "Would you hire the people you have knowing what you know now?" He sees how uncomfortable the question makes them. So where does it fall apart?

When it comes to creating a team environment, the first mistake happens before a hire is even made. Teamwork is a daily active creation that starts by looking beyond a candidate's experience and asking,

"Does this person seem like they would be a good fit and teammate for the culture we are creating?"

Of course, fit is just the first criteria. You need to be sure someone can do the job, which is not the same as having experience. Ryan learned that the hard way when he started his leadership career. His hiring criteria was competitive guys who played sports and showed up polished, rocking a nice suit (don't judge). He was particularly enamored of one guy who played DI football at a major university. Ryan took the guy to dinner and thought, *This guy is going to kill it.*

"He looked the part and said all the right things, so I hired him. That guy couldn't close a door let alone a sale," Ryan says, shaking his head at the memory. "I let hiring people 'like me' get in the way of doing the interview I needed to do to find out he was a good fit and couldn't do the job. Sure, he was competitive and had discipline, but I didn't probe beyond the surface to discover that wasn't enough. I didn't do a thorough enough job vetting him as a candidate and giving him a realistic job preview to ascertain that he was the best person for the job. I should've had him in the office the day after dinner and walked him through a day in the life inside the business. Asked him questions. Challenged him on how he would approach the opportunity. That was a shortsighted move on my part. I eventually fired him, but it cost me a lot of valuable time and hurt us in that territory for a couple of years. Big mistake."

But once you're sure about the ability to do the job, focus on fit.

When the Cowboys charged Chad with leading a search for a senior position in the organization, the first questions were about whether a person would fit with the culture of the leadership team, not experience: Could they find someone who could get in the trenches *and* had the personality to build strong relationships? Who could give of themselves and who everyone would enjoy being around? The same was true when Chad and his team hired people to sell the Cowboys' new stadium. In fact, they brought in some of the less experienced people because they knew they had the personality to fit the culture of the team. They had set up expectations for career development during the interview process and could see from a person's reaction and body language if they understood.

The other major factor for Chad was likability: "If I'm going to put a person in a cube next to my team, I have an obligation to those people to make sure this person isn't an arrogant jerk and who will disrupt our team culture. No other mistake I have made makes people look at me and wonder why I did that then when I've made a hiring decision like that."

Note: *Fit*, like the words *people* and *human*, shouldn't mean *same*. Ryan made the mistake early in his professional career by hiring people who looked and sounded like him, and that blind spot cost him as a young manager. He didn't need another him. He needed to find and embrace people who added value where he couldn't—who connected to people not like him and could see, do, and understand things he couldn't as part of a diverse team and culture that embraced difference but shared the same goals. We need to invite diversity on all levels (experience, thought, background, identity, gender, etc.) into our culture and then make sure to include them. If there is alignment from a professional value, cultural, and goals perspective, any other differences should be welcome. Without that, your team or company not only diminishes its reach but might never see how limited it is as you create echo chambers and perpetuate confirmation bias. Any resistance to this is just fear and ego talking.

Great leaders and organizations get that ego is a virus when it comes to the team environment and try never to let the infection in no matter how much experience and talent the person has. Ryan never saw a better example of that in a company he worked with than the Mayo Clinic. The company attracts patients from around the world. But patients come and go. What about the people that work there every day? That's why teamwork is a core value. "They've codified that as setting their ego aside, serving the needs of the patient first, and working in concert with each other," Ryan says. "They refuse to hire people with massive egos as a result. Doesn't matter if you are the leading cardiac surgeon in the world. No God complexes. Those people can go work somewhere else."

At the Mayo Clinic, of course, teamwork can be a matter of life and death. Yours probably isn't. But employees who fit a people-first culture in any business are always willing to be the teammates they learned to be by making sacrifices, sharing, caring for each other, and stepping in for the good of the team. That gives a team life. Bad teammates don't share. They are selfish. They hoard information. They obsess over who gets credit. They don't help. They gossip. They complain. They bring the energy down. Shutting all that down and not allowing it to spread is on you as the leader. Create a culture that allows that to happen—one that codifies and values it. That lifts people up, engages them, and celebrates the work they do.

CELEBRATE PROGRESS (NOT JUST OUTCOMES)

Progress is happiness. People want to feel like they have momentum, like they are contributing to something that is headed in the right direction. The best leaders look for opportunities for recognition on all levels to reinforce what's going right on a team. The easiest place to start doing that is in meetings.

"Too many meetings are run the same way," says Ryan. "They are about problems and resolution, not success: What are we going to do to turn around or solve this problem? Why did this customer complain, client leave, mistakes get made, etc. Instead, starting meetings with a story about progress, impact, or teamwork is leadership gold. Those stories are treasure troves for recognition and reinforcing the right behavior."

Notice that Ryan said telling a story about outcomes is only one of three ways to start a meeting, not the only way. If it is, you are focusing too much on performance and profitability and not enough on what people are doing to get to those things. After all, results usually speak for themselves and are recognized formally elsewhere. In sales, there is a real-time dashboard, contests, annual trips for the biggest sellers, salesperson of the month, and plenty of opportunity to recognize the result. Go ahead and be generous with that recognition when it is warranted. But recognition in meetings—stories celebrating progress—can have even more impact, boost morale, provide an opportunity for learning, and connect people to something larger than themselves.

Informal recognition of small wins is also essential, which Ryan calls "on the spot" or "real-time" recognition. "That means it's in the flow of business, not at a meeting or a performance review. It's about saying, 'I heard what you said in that meeting, and it was great,' or 'You are setting up a big win for us, and I see how hard you are going at it.' Then there's just small touch points of stopping by someone's desk and saying thank you for the time you put in—that you noticed and are grateful. It all becomes part of how you operate and is connected to spending time with your people. It's not something most leaders keep top of mind, because it seems like such a small thing."

Chad couldn't agree more and makes it a point to ensure his leaders are operating that way: "I ask them over coffee how they think they're doing with recognition. I reinforce it constantly by example. I need it to become part of their routines." He also uses recognition moments to notice if a teammate is slipping into a negative place: "When I see reps pout because someone else made the sale, I pull that person into my office and ask, 'What's the problem? Your body language when we were celebrating didn't look so great.' If they tell me they are struggling, we can talk about what they're going through but I also ask, 'How do you think that person felt when you're sitting there like that?' I confront the poor sportsmanship head-on. Being a good teammate means caring for the person who sits next to you. That's why being genuinely happy for their success is so important. Sharing success reinforces all the other steps and leads to more sharing."

"This is something a low percentage of leaders do," Ryan adds. "That takes courage to shut that down and be compassionate. Seeing that happen gets around to the team and gets baked into a culture. And I guarantee you if that person showed up at a few more celebrations and acted that way, they would be gone."

Unfortunately, there are a lot of leaders who only focus on what's going wrong, bosses like Chad's early in his career who bitched at the team if they didn't get results two hours after they got in. Frank Pacetta called that a "public flogging."

"Can you imagine what we said when we got back to our desks after that?" Chad recalls. "Every curse you can imagine. We were immersed in negativity. It's amazing how fast that turns into negativity toward each other. You start hearing things like, 'I'm super sick of this person doing this,' or 'All that person over there does is complain.' I resolved to do everything I could to make sure I never let that happen as a leader."

TEAR DOWN SILOS

When Ryan does research on an organization in advance of his work with them, issues of cross-company communication and creating connections across the organization almost always rise to the top: "Most companies are siloed in some way. That often means critical information isn't being shared, people get protective of their turf, and people aren't encouraged to communicate across the organization. In that scenario, leaders might have great team environments, but they aren't working for an organization that works as a team or puts the company objectives first."

Even for smaller teams and companies, this expectation of a consistent and connected culture becomes imperative, especially as you grow. "For a long time, I was managing sales teams with very specific requirements," Chad says. We didn't have to work across teams. We didn't see the value in it. But when I have eight people running departments for me? Most businesses already have silos between their teams and other departments. We don't need them between our people. I need them not only to break down the silos between them but within their teams. I need the culture to be consistent. We can't have different rules for different people on our teams. We can't treat people differently."

That's especially true when it comes to departments and divisions you don't regularly interact with. Every team and department in an organization has a reputation, and every interaction shapes that reputation. Sales may not have a daily need for legal, HR, or operations, but if you're a jackass when you do need them or you cop an attitude when they take longer than you expected on something, what do you think those departments think about your team? They feel undervalued and underappreciated. That's unacceptable.

"How motivated do you think those departments will be when you really need something next or it's on a Saturday, and you need to push a deal through?" asks Chad. "They're not coming in. They're not helping you any more than they have to. We have to treat them the way we want to be treated. Everything we do is about external and internal service as a team. How fast we respond and how well we respond. That's why when I get a call from another department that says my people pulled some BS, I pull the whole team in and address it."

Ryan saw plenty of this in his ad agency days and offers a step toward a solution before problems even start—one that goes back to one of the first tactics on this list: Have at least two meetings outside your immediate area business every month. Selling must be a company-wide team sport. Go for coffee with someone on your level who is in marketing or accounting or accounts payable or IT. Extend your network into the business and create those cross functional relationships and understand the priorities of these other areas. Spend time with and get to know each other. Make it a priority and an expectation.

PREPARE FOR IMPACT:
BUILD A TEAM ENVIRONMENT

KEYS TO SUCCESS
- Focus on fit.
- Celebrate progress (not just outcomes).
- Tear down silos.

ASK
- How do you recognize what's going right?
- How am I fostering a team environment?
- How am I breaking down the silos between people and teams to drive collaboration throughout the organization?

6. Create Connection—Have Fun!

We had one guiding principle when we started writing this book: make it fun. And it was. It was also hard work, time consuming, challenging, and intense at times, and we had high expectations for our performance and the performance of our team who helped us put it together. Anything worth doing has elements of all of that. But having fun in pursuit of something meaningful is what kept us going. We looked forward to working on it just like we do when we are at our day jobs. The relationships and shared experiences that result from putting people together in a culture that values connection, collaboration, and celebrating progress in pursuit of a meaningful cause helps keep everyone engaged, no matter what kind of work you're doing.

This tactic is about *purpose*—both your purpose as a leader and the sense of purpose others feel when they are aligned in pursuit of a noble cause that is much larger than themselves. The fulfillment that comes from genuine connection and fun often serve as the foundation for engagement, relationships, and performance. Most leaders value purpose for its commercial value to reputation and the bottom line, and they are right: There will always be a symbiotic relationship between how people feel about their jobs and how customers feel about the business. But it's easy to miss that what matters to employees is the experience—the *meaning*—they find in their work and each other. They want to feel like they belong and are contributing to something larger than themselves. According to McKinsey, 70 percent of employees say "their sense of purpose is defined by

Organizations that connect employees to their culture increase employee performance by up to 37% and retention by up to 36%.[30]

their work,"[31] and according to PricewaterhouseCoopers' study of purpose in the workplace, the top two priorities of employees are finding meaning in their day-to-day work and having a strong sense of community[32]—two things valued significantly lower by leaders who valued reputation for growth and innovation above all else.

KEYS TO SUCCESS

- Make connecting intentional.
- Be a catalyst for deepening relationships.
- Inject work with laughter.

MAKE CONNECTING INTENTIONAL

"Turn around and just look," Ryan said to Chad as he got on the bus. We were in Austin for a Cowboys' leadership retreat. Ryan had worked with the team earlier in the day and joined everyone for a happy hour earned from a long day of learning and discussion. Now they were on the bus together heading to the legendary Salt Lick BBQ.

Chad turned around. Everyone was laughing and talking with each other, music blasting and beers in hand from happy hour. "This is work," Chad said, smiling. "This is what I am talking about."

That moment in Austin was a perfect example of why Chad fights so hard for the budget and time for sales retreats: "At every point in my leadership career, I have heard some version of, 'I'm not paying twenty thousand dollars for people to go to a party,'" Chad says. "But when I explain the value those parties have for our people and share the notes I get from them thanking me, no one questions it. Spending money to get out of the office, whether it is presenting the business, blowing off some steam, or anywhere in between deepens engagement. The buy-in and the camaraderie that result are worth it all. It gets even more important when you have multiple teams across an organization or need to bring together different departments. You need them to keep cross pollinating and cross communicating to keep those silos from going back up."

Ryan longed for this connection to others when the pandemic shut down his business. He believes so deeply in fun as a basis for that connection that when he cofounded his new company, ImpactEleven, fun became the foundation of one of its guiding principles: "Dance Like Nobody's Watching." As Ryan notes, "That principle says we prioritize fun. We are intent on enjoying the journey. We reject politics and BS. We are creating lives we love. And we want all those things for the people we work with."

That's what we mean by making connecting intentional. You need to have a culture that allows genuine moments of fun to happen inside and outside the business, constantly and consistently, both structured and unstructured. Do that and people will come in genuinely *wanting* to have fun spending time with each other, not because they *have to* (compliance). Don't do that and efforts to make it fun can feel contrived and actually become a joke.

Note: This key to success can be harder to execute in a distributed workforce, like Ryan's at ImpactEleven, or a hybrid or virtual company where not everyone comes into an office. That only reinforces the importance of making the most of every in-person opportunity— meetings, conferences, retreats, and beyond. These are ways for people to connect and feel like they are contributing to something bigger than themselves.

BE A CATALYST FOR DEEPENING RELATIONSHIPS

Ryan saw that Chad understood the need for him and his people to see each other in different ways and enjoy being around each other.

"Chad understands that in a high-performance environment, the benefit is not in the moment but later when shit goes wrong, a person needs a little help, or someone has an issue they need to deal with," Ryan says. "Then the team's reaction is, 'I got you. We're in this together.' When that happens, everything about work is that much better. People are better teammates. They help each other. In the absence of fun, all you have is people going to work. There is no connection. There is no purpose."

Chad had years of experience in that kind of culture—where purpose is defined by performance alone—before he became a leader. He had one boss who was basically antifun. Every time he came into a room it was all business all the time. He'd gather them together and start going down his list *boom, boom, boom.* No, "How you doing?" No small talk. Come to work for eight to ten hours a day, do your job, leave. He didn't see the point in anything else, let alone enjoying your time in the office. But why would anybody want to do anything for that much time and not enjoy it? The sad part was this boss wasn't exceptional. We've been in dozens of offices in which people will tell us, "Our boss doesn't socialize with the staff," or "He's just our boss."

To build a team, leaders must spend time ensuring the opposite of that happens—and see influencing culture as one of the most important parts of their jobs. They need to understand that relationships are as important inside work to our overall happiness as those outside. That love and caring of others are at the heart of every relationship and essential to performance. That understanding is a big reason behind why Gallup has been leading with the same question of employees in its employee engagement research for more than three decades: Do you have a best friend at work? This engagement question from Gallup serves to reinforce that people who do have a best friend at work are more engaged, productive, and innovative—and have more fun![33]

INJECT WORK WITH LAUGHTER

No one was ever laughing in those antifun offices of Chad's. At the Cowboys, even in their business report meetings in the formal big boardroom with the four Joneses at the end, one of them will say something super funny, and the whole place is laughing.

"That's a perfect representation of the culture for me: high expectations, high pressure, desire to be the best in what we do, and enjoying each other and laughing *together*," says Chad. "That sets that tone of the culture for the entire organization. The fun is already baked in. People want to get together to do an activity—form a sports team, raise money for a cause, work out together, or just grab a few beers across the street. That kind of unstructured connection happens organically. Then you create structured experiences like those retreats. We also fold fun into recognition and celebrations, and we make sure we live it in our meetings, emails, what we display around the office. Some of it can even be corny and goofy. But people love it. What happens is the people start to grow together. Relationships start to form. Friendships start to form—lifelong friendships."

That's what it was like for Ryan at the advertising agency before he started his second career. The culture there was to have dinner together no matter where they were: "You'd go into a city and have a meeting and have dinner together with the people who worked there. Those dinners are a big reason I remain friends with those people. To this day, if I am in Louisville, I will make time to have dinner and catch up with my dear friend Don Sabatino, who I worked with years ago, because we were united by something bigger than us, enjoyed our time together, and ultimately developed a relationship that transcended the work."

PREPARE FOR IMPACT:
CREATE CONNECTION–HAVE FUN!

KEYS TO SUCCESS
- Make connecting intentional.
- Be a catalyst for deepening relationships.
- Inject work with laughter.

ASK
- What do you want the work experience to feel like regardless of where the work is getting done?
- Who creates the opportunities for connection? How do you make time for connections in your workplace, especially if it's a hybrid environment or everyone is working remotely?
- Did you have fun today? Now ask your team: Did you have fun today?

7. Be Vulnerable

"Capable of being physically or emotionally wounded." That's the dictionary definition of *vulnerability*, which makes it sound like a weakness. In leadership, it's not. It's the greatest strength you can have; it becomes a catalyst for creating authentic and meaningful connections with people. Brené Brown calls vulnerability "emotional exposure," the "birthplace of love, belonging, joy, courage,

Only 20% of employees say leaders openly share the challenges they're facing. 21% say leaders never or rarely openly share them.[34]

empathy, and creativity," and the "source of hope, empathy, accountability, and authenticity." Wow. We couldn't have said it better ourselves, so we didn't. That's the kind of vulnerability every leader should aspire to.

Admitting you don't know everything, acknowledging you got something wrong, genuinely apologizing, talking about your struggles . . . we can't begin to list all the things that go into being vulnerable as a leader. So we picked one way: telling stories.

Storytelling is a master leadership competency. Delivered authentically, stories are among the most profoundly human things we can do. This goes way beyond using stories to sell stuff and sell yourself to your customers that was a part of the 30 Steps. Knowing someone's life story—and sharing yours—is the foundation for depth in relationships and helps build trust.

Stories that open us up and allow us to be vulnerable are treasure troves for that level of engagement and reinforcing the right behavior to get where we're going. Go ahead: look inside yourself, open your heart, fight through your discomfort, and tell your people a story. Stories from the heart engage us and connect us emotionally, and since emotions rule our behavior, the stories we share can be used to:

- reinforce a shared vision of the future and help us imagine all that is possible.
- connect us to our shared humanity.
- make an idea we have or work we are doing resonate.

- allow us to understand and share what really matters to each other.
- make us more likable and, if not nice, at least nicer to be around.
- enable us to see ourselves in another.

KEYS TO SUCCESS

- Be authentically you.
- Reconcile your truths.
- Bind everyone to shared values.

BE AUTHENTICALLY YOU

Turns out there is a scientific explanation for stories' effect on our behavior. Dr. Paul Zak, director of the Center for Neuroeconomics Studies at Claremont Graduate University, has done groundbreaking research on how stories shape our brains. His lab found that when the brain synthesizes oxytocin, the neurochemical responsible for empathy and narrative transportation, people are "more trustworthy, generous, charitable, and compassionate" (he calls it "the moral molecule"). Not every story releases oxytocin, but those told with meaning and context and emotional resonance that draw the listener in do. In one experiment around public service ads, Zak and his research partners found the release of oxytocin generated 57 percent more donations, 56 percent more money in total, and 17 percent greater concern for those in the ad.[35]

But you didn't need science to know all that.

You've known the power of stories since you were a child and asked someone to read or tell you one, over and over again. Most of us remember at least one lesson those stories taught us, and they continue to inspire us to do better. The same is true when we become adults. Frank Pacetta became our hero because he told stories like no one else. What he was saying wasn't unique in the world of business books, but the stories he told were and they bound us to him for life.

We see this book as one long story of our relationship and journey through business so far, and truth be told, it tested our willingness to be vulnerable. We haven't always liked what we said when we saw it written down:

I sound like an asshole in that story.

I'm a little aggressive in the way I'm depicted there.

I don't want to tell that to people.

I think I sound egotistical.

But that's what being vulnerable is all about. We'll never reach the level of vulnerability Brené Brown lays out if we don't face that discomfort and share it openly. Remember: it's not fake until you make it; it's face it until you make it. That's vulnerability. That's part of the reason we needed to get comfortable sharing everything we have in this book—that we blew that call, handled that situation badly, or acted like a jerk.

We don't like how it feels sometimes—like Chad admitting Ryan was right and ending eight-to-six office hours after Ryan called him "suit and tie" or taking his only L in our annual challenge. Ryan in particular flinches when he shares stories about his early days and letting his ego reign unchecked, but that's because he knows ego is the killer of more than a great story and could have easily cost him his job as a leader. But that's how we know we're allowing ourselves to be vulnerable. Putting our stories in the service of that vulnerability encourages others to share theirs and creates connections and engagement that last a lifetime.

RECONCILE YOUR TRUTHS

Being vulnerable as a leader requires elevating your confidence and humility at the same time. That isn't easy. But leaders who achieve that are going to have some dynamic results. They are going to garner support in times of adversity and challenge. They are going to help their teams be resilient and push through obstacles.

This doesn't mean revealing your deepest darkest childhood traumas unless that's the purpose. Your stories can have influence without spilling your guts. Just know that a story is more than an anecdote (a single account of something that happens). A story links several events or pieces of history or events together into a narrative that can and should entertain us, celebrate success, teach a lesson, and more.

For example, Chad was talking to a group of young people and made a point to share what it was like for him when he was where they are now. "I didn't just talk about career development and my successes. I admitted I was scared and worried. I told them how I thought I was going to fail when I started and had no idea what to do. I told them about fighting doubts that something would work and then turning that doubt into belief. Afterward, many of them came up to me and said how helpful it was to hear someone in my position share that he struggled. Insecure and ego-driven leaders can't do this. Even if they are successful now, they think it makes them look weak."

BIND EVERYONE TO SHARED VALUES

Consider how the Cowboys used stories to connect with the team's core values—teamwork, integrity, excellence, community, passion—at its annual company-wide "State of the Union." Before the meeting, an email went out asking anyone to submit names of people who best exemplified one of those values along with a story why. The key was that story; it had to be specific. The executive team reviewed all of them and picked five, one for each value. At the State of the Union, the Cowboys honored those people by reading their stories aloud to everyone.

"It was hard to get through," Chad says. "Everyone there from the Jones family on down was cheering or crying. It was an emotional moment that bound us to each other."

That's the key word: *bind*. The power of stories in business is they bind us: we are here, we are going to get there, and we will make it together. In fact, the shared values that are the guiding principles of ImpactEleven, Ryan's new company, clearly tell a story about the culture the moment you read them: Play Jazz, Not Classical; Do Less Better; Give Generously; Don't Keep Score; With a Little Help from My Friends; Reach for Eleven; Dance Like Nobody's Watching; Smoother than a Fresh Jar of Skippy; and Leave It Better than We Found It. Even if you don't know exactly what they mean, you understand something about ImpactEleven: That this is decidedly not a typical corporate environment, and you're going to have to open yourself up to a different way of thinking about how and whether your story fits.

"These principles and all our core beliefs and mission are unique and germane to ImpactEleven," says Ryan. "You read them, and you know who we are, how we roll, how we think about each other. You know our expectations and the impact we expect our work to contribute to the world. You know how we work. Can every company do them like we do? Perhaps not. But the purpose of our principles and beliefs are at their core the same as Chad's at the Cowboys and what Chad does every day in using these nine tactics: To make people feel what it means to be a part of the team and the company by living them every day. That's why he's one of those leaders prepared to lead beyond the pandemic into the new world of work."

> ## PREPARE FOR IMPACT:
> # BE VULNERABLE
>
> **KEYS TO SUCCESS**
> - Be authentically you.
> - Reconcile your truths.
> - Bind everyone to shared values.
>
> **ASK**
> - When was the last time you told your people a story that opened you up to your people?
> - How well do your people know you?
> - What are the shared values of your team? How do you learn them and live them? Can you tell a story around them?

8. Have Tough Conversations

Your people know you care about their development. You've gone for coffee and practiced transparency. You've built a team environment that is fun and safe. You've been vulnerable. You're having great conversations with your people as a result. You're ready for the tough ones, right? *Right*? Hey, where'd you go? Tough conversations trigger the same response in even the best leaders that danger does:

> Top reasons leaders often don't have difficult conversations with employees: fear of conflict, thinking it's unkind, and not making the conversations a priority.[36]

fight or flight. Maybe not the trembling, dilated pupils, and flushed skin, but definitely the rapid heartbeat and breathing. It's natural to want to avoid the stress and take flight, not face what you fear head-on. Don't—and don't let your people do it either.

> ### KEYS TO SUCCESS
> - Avoid avoiding.
> - Have the courage to hold yourself accountable.
> - Have the courage to say goodbye.

AVOID AVOIDING

A Harris Poll commissioned by Interact Studio found that more than one-third of all leaders are uncomfortable giving feedback and talking about performance when they think employees "might respond badly." That same survey showed that 69 percent of leaders are "uncomfortable" communicating with their employees *at all*.[37] Consider that number against the Gallup poll cited in tactic four that shows two-thirds of employees are disengaged at work. We know correlation is not causation, but it is interesting that leaders' discomfort communicating with their people and the number of disengaged employees match up. Not surprising, either, which is why these tactics (like the 30 Steps) place a priority on communication.

What does surprise us is that so few leaders report being uncomfortable delivering feedback and talking about performance. It's probably even higher when it comes to the tough conversations based on the leaders Ryan has worked with. "One of the biggest leadership challenges of our time is that everything really difficult goes unaddressed.

Few people, not just leaders, are willing and know how to deal with problems, bad news, and personal conflict head-on. Instead of confronting people and problems directly, mitigating differences, seeking understanding, being transparent, accepting the consequences, and *doing* something, they avoid these conversations, cover up or ignore the situation, and hope the problem just goes away. Unfortunately, avoided conflict only grows."

Chad takes the opposite approach: He welcomes the tough conversations as healthy conflict in the present to avoid tension in the future. He walks into a fire the second he sees it smoldering. Chad also provides training to help leaders learn to confront situations like he has and, if it is their responsibility, makes them practice what they learned. If leaders come to Chad for help dealing with another person or a client, he will tell them, "I cannot help you. You need to talk to that person yourself." He then tells them to come back after they do and tell him how it went. In other words, Chad leaves them no choice but to have the courage to take responsibility and hold themselves accountable to whatever the problem or situation requires.

No attacking. No blaming. No complaining.

HAVE THE COURAGE TO HOLD YOURSELF ACCOUNTABLE

Early in his leadership career, one of Chad's bosses sent an email to Chad and the rest of his team ripping one of Chad's most dedicated guys to shreds after he made a mistake. There was no safety for this guy, and he came into Chad's office destroyed. Chad told him not to worry about it—that he was not as bad as that email made him out to be. But the email was out there, and now everyone in the office was talking about it. It took weeks for Chad to talk his guy off the ledge. Chad was angry at his boss the entire time. But he didn't have the courage to say something, until the anger that gnawed inside him was too much.

Chad scheduled a meeting and immediately got into it. He reminded his boss about the email and said, "I don't think you understood the power of your words. This guy never interacts with you. He may have shaken your hand one time. And then he gets an email from you ripping him to shreds with cuss words? He is devastated, and now we're supposed to get good work out of him and motivate him? When you say something to someone around here, it means everything to them."

Chad didn't see his boss's response coming: "Well, why didn't you come say something to me sooner? If somebody sees something around here they don't like, it has to be addressed right away."

Chad did not take kindly to that response. "I thought it was BS. He didn't believe what he was saying and was trying to squirm out of being called out." But soon he saw the lesson learned. "I'm at fault for not having the courage to address it a month ago."

Whether mistakes, role clarity, unclear expectations, or anything else, resolve to find the courage to embrace the tough conversations quickly. Seek help if you need it. Set your ego aside and consider working with other leaders. The Cowboys have operationalized that as part of the "accountability partner" program we also discussed in step 5 of the 30 Steps: Two people are accountable to ask questions about what they are doing and tell each other when they're doing something that's not good for the team. You see something, you share it. That's your responsibility. Now deal with it. What can you do?

HAVE THE COURAGE TO SAY GOODBYE

What do you do with a top performer who is also an asshole? Ryan got this question at the end of a presentation, and he knew why the person asked. It's hard to lose those numbers, so you look for a reason to avoid the obvious character issues. But reason does not lead to the truth. It leads to a story designed to avoid tough conversations. Ryan's answer: "If you've given that person a chance to turn it around, he's gotta go."

Ryan spoke from experience, not just research on this issue, as he reflected on one of his biggest weaknesses as a new manager. "I didn't have the courage to confront things. I was conflict avoidant. I placed a premium on results to the detriment of the effect on my culture. That was a rookie mistake. What I should've done was taken a hard stance, completed my hundred-day observation, had my one-on-ones, called people on their shit instead of being afraid of the perceived conflict in those hard conversations."

The person who asked Ryan the question at the presentation was doing the same thing: Focusing on the numbers, not the people whose performance was being affected by the asshole. "When you work so hard to build a great culture, the one thing you can never allow is a bad teammate, no matter how good that person is," Ryan told his questioner. "No one is above the team you have created. The conversation only gets tougher if the person is not only a top performer but someone you like and/or consider a friend. But it has to happen."

Chad knows this whole situation all too well. It happened with one of his favorite employees of all time. Chad hired him as an entry-level account executive, and he became one of the best salespeople he had ever seen in the industry. He sold by himself what the other five people on his team sold *combined*. Chad started moving him up the ladder and eventually into a choice leadership role. That's when things started to fall apart.

"He was running roughshod over everyone he interacted with," Chad recalls. "He was aggressive. No one could operate at his abnormal pace nor did they need to. I told him to slow down if just for his own health. His response was, 'I love to work. I don't have a family. I want to be here at six thirty.'" Chad tried to work around that with him. He explained he could be here at that time, but he didn't have to send the twenty emails his people were waking up to and now have anxiety the whole day: "They *do* have families. You're at your desk firing off these emails, and they're walking their dog and getting their kids ready for school. How do you think that makes them feel? The problem went way beyond those emails, but I figured they were a way to get into the bigger issues. But his expectations remained unreasonable and his inability to put people first remained awful."

Chad waited for his young leader to turn things around until he'd had enough. He took him out of the office one morning and let him have it: "I love you. But you don't think I will fire you? You are wrong. No one is bigger than this team and what we are doing here. You are fucking this up. Big time."

"No one *likes* those conversations," Ryan says. "I hate them. I've had sleepless nights on the cusp of them. Because I'm conflict avoidant, it makes it even harder for me to get up the courage. But Chad welcomes tough conversations and healthy conflict in the service of what he is trying to create. That's what great leaders do. They have the courage to say, 'I love you, *and* I'll miss you if you don't turn it around.'"

Which is exactly what Chad's employee did. By having that tough conversation, Chad did not let it get to the point where he needed to fire him. Instead, this leader used the tough conversation to think about how he was being perceived by others, shift his mindset, and take responsibility for his success. In fact, he has become one of the best sales and business leaders Chad has worked with. Sure, he continues to work at a pace unlike anyone Chad knows, but he worked hard not to have those same expectations of everyone around him.

What happened with Chad's person is the point of the tough conversation: To address issues and problems *before* they become unsolvable. Have the tough conversation early and you at least give people a chance to turn it around and succeed. No, it doesn't always work out that way. Some people don't care what you have to say or won't listen. Some people never change or can't get better. Sometimes you will need to move out people who just don't have the skills or desire to do the job you need them to do. If that happens and you've been doing the majority of these tactics, they know, and the conversation shouldn't be a surprise to them even if that lack of surprise doesn't necessarily make it any easier.

PREPARE FOR IMPACT:
HAVE TOUGH CONVERSATIONS

KEYS TO SUCCESS
- Avoid avoiding.
- Have the courage to hold yourself accountable.
- Have the courage to say goodbye.

ASK
- What conversations are you avoiding because they make you uncomfortable?
- How can you hold yourself accountable to have those conversations?
- When you avoided saying goodbye to someone for too long, what was the result?

9. Be Decisive

The best leaders have a healthy action orientation for executing plans and achieving their goals quickly and efficiently. They act with courage and confidence and own the outcomes. They don't suffer from analysis paralysis. They know how to weigh all the options and information efficiently and "make the call" without doubt, questioning, and blame if their call goes sideways or turns out to be wrong.

Research shows a 95% correlation between companies that excel at making and executing key decisions and those with top-tier financial results, whether measured in terms of revenue growth, return on capital, or total shareholder return.[38]

KEYS TO SUCCESS

- Ask, "What's the worst thing that could happen?"
- Have the courage of your convictions.
- Remember where all this started.

ASK, "WHAT'S THE WORST THING THAT COULD HAPPEN?"

There is never a perfect time to make a big decision. You need to do your due diligence and gather as much information as you can. Talk to people who know all the players in the situation. Talk to your people openly and transparently to get their reaction. Leverage your advisors and mentors. Ask questions and listen to what they have to say. Let them challenge you and then support you. But after all that, know you'll still have to look at and extrapolate from incomplete data to make the call. And it might not go well.

Don't let that stop you.

Indecisiveness is the problem child of insecurity. If you can't make decisions quickly and decisively and stand behind them, that's a big barrier to performance. It frustrates your team and leads to missed opportunities. Creating safety is essential for this tactic: If you have created safety for yourself and your team to take risks and make mistakes, you'll be able to make the call and accept the consequences. If you believe in yourself, then you really don't worry about the consequences; you embrace them. In fact, you usually end up regretting the things you don't try a whole lot more than the things that perhaps didn't work out like you expected.

"Indecisiveness comes down to fear setting, and I'll say it again: our brains are wired for safety and comfort," says Ryan. "Asking, 'What's the worst thing that could happen to me with this decision?' is a way forward through discomfort. Often the wrong call is reversible and recoverable, which helps mitigate the fear factor. Worst case, if I made a series of detrimental decisions and lost my job, I needed to be confident that I would bounce out of that and within twelve months know the odds were very high that I would recover and be back where I was. That even if I made a big mistake, it was recoverable. That's what allowed me to make the decision to start my own business. I lived with the worst possibilities in my mind and found they were never worse than the opportunities. As a result, even when I struggled getting the business off the ground, I never regretted the decision or beat myself up for making the call. Over time that made me a lot more confident."

HAVE THE COURAGE OF YOUR CONVICTIONS

As we matured in our leadership roles and learned to confidently express our opinions, both of us became a bit challenging and aggressive in taking an opposing view on critical business decisions. *This is my thing. I believe this to be true. I know it will work for this organization.*

We wanted to align what we needed with what our bosses and the organizations wanted. Our best bosses enjoyed the challenge. They heard us when we challenged or asked questions about a course of action or a strategic decision, and they answered and defended their positions with equal conviction. We didn't always see our challenges lead to changes, but we sure tried, and we lined up behind those actions and decisions even when a decision went another way.

That said, a time will come when you must choose between the expectations of your boss and the team or organization and being true to your values and who you are. That happened for Chad as he was about to build the team to sell the Cowboys' stadium. Jerry Jones wanted Chad to hire some local people experienced in selling other things in Dallas, like mortgages, houses, and cars; they could call their customers and sell premium seat licenses to all of them. Chad was given three names Jerry thought would be perfect. He looked them over. Talented salespeople, for sure, but he couldn't see any of them fitting his vision for the team the Cowboys wanted and needed. Three weeks into the job of a lifetime, he had a huge philosophical difference with the owner.

Chad decided to talk to Jerry's sons first. He explained he couldn't do what their dad wanted and asked them what he should do. "They were a little taken aback at first. Then they asked why I didn't want to hire those people. I explained how they were not going to fit on the team the Cowboys hired me to create. They told me to write all of what I said down in an email. They would make sure their dad read it.

Chad wrote six paragraphs in an email about the team he wanted and the Cowboys needed. He felt passionate about every word and didn't know what was going to happen. But the Jones brothers kept their promise, and soon after Chad sent the email, Jerry called Chad in for a meeting. "Jerry had read every word. He remained super passionate about his way and respected that I was super passionate about mine. He asked me questions. He debated with me a bit. Finally, he decided, 'All right, do it your way.' I think he saw me really believe and have confidence in what I wanted to deliver the results we both wanted and expected for the team. It was a defining moment for me. I made the decision to stand my ground for the people I really believed in, and Jerry did the same with me."

Simply put, having the confidence to stand up for what you believe and the people you serve not only earns respect but makes you inclusive. That willingness to test your beliefs against those of people who have different experiences, opinions, methods, and tactics than you gives you confidence and allows you and your team to execute in ways that best serve them and the organization. No greater way to show you truly understand what it means to put people first.

REMEMBER WHERE ALL THIS STARTED

Chad's previous story brings us back not only to the philosophy of this list but also the first question we asked about the 30 Steps: How important is this to you? The more these tactics are genuinely part of your leadership story, the closer you get to building that functional high-performance culture that people can't wait to get to work to be a part of. The kind of culture and job that launches people into the careers of their dreams.

Decide to do something about it.

PREPARE FOR IMPACT:
BE DECISIVE

KEYS TO SUCCESS

- Ask, "What's the worst thing that could happen?"
- Have the courage of your convictions.
- Remember where all this started.

ASK

- How do you show your decisiveness?
- How do you stand up for what you believe in deeply and know something is right?

CHAPTER 7

LEAD YOUR LEGACY

BOTH OF US HAVE had bosses who would not understand the importance of these leadership tactics, but that is not a recipe for disaster. If your vision for what you want for your team is out of alignment with the organization, don't blame or complain. Work even harder to *act*. Focus on the things that are within your sphere of influence and control and create a microculture on your team in which people can contribute and thrive. Lead by example by treating your people the way you would want to be treated. You don't need to challenge the values of the company to construct a microculture that you and your team look forward to working in—just deliver on (and exceed) expectations while you do. Then, as you deliver better results, see if you can cascade the effect of that microculture up, down, and across the rest of the organization.

Even in the best organizations, things are always going to happen you may not agree with or like. You won't like some decisions. You might take a stand, lose the debate, and watch the team or company go in a different direction. You might find somebody else gets recognized and/or takes the credit for work you were a big part of. You will see deals go sideways. Someone will screw something up. This is in addition to stuff you can't control any more than you can control the weather.

What you *always* have control of is how you show up—for others *and* yourself. Doing this effectively requires what Ryan calls an "inside-out" approach to leadership—to do the inner work as well as the outer work to serve others.

"I initially struggled in leadership because I was so insecure and let my ego get in the way," Ryan says. "To get past that, I had to take a closer look inside myself, confront the problem of me, and commit to my healing, growth, and development. I had to acknowledge that I am first and foremost the source of my problems—the barrier to engagement, growth, and fulfillment for others. To get out of my own way, I started working on myself and still commit to and continue that today. I practice immersive learning. I schedule personal growth retreats. I work with a coach. I have also learned how to step away from the work and unplug. By improving my relationship with myself, I improved my ability to develop better relationships with others."

Starting your inner work begins with self-awareness, asking yourself questions like:

- Where do I need to grow to become a better leader?
- How am I learning, evolving, and improving every day?
- Who am I becoming?

Leaders are learners, so stay in the learning lane just like you did in the 30 Steps. Encourage your own development at least five hours per week. Read. Write. Grow. What that growth leads to is adaptability, presence, curiosity, confidence, humility, and self-love. That's what this inner work is all about. Too many leaders struggle with this or avoid it altogether. They want to fight the status quo but then only do the work to change when the pain of what they are doing becomes greater than the fear of change. Don't wait. Fight through the fear of the unknown. Embrace uncertainty and risk.

Look inside and *disrupt yourself before the marketplace or your competition does it for you.*

Remember: Everything you do every day is observed. Great leaders realize the impact their presence has on everybody around them. If you show up as the best version of who you are, you give yourself the best opportunity to meet people where they are. We all have heard that leadership is an act of service, but you must serve yourself as well as the people you answer to and who answer to you. It's hard to help other people become the best they can be when you're not doing that for yourself. Start now. Your legacy depends on it. Build a healthy relationship with yourself.

Yes, your legacy. No matter what kind of company you work for or where you are in your career trajectory, you don't have to wait to leave your legacy. In fact, you started doing it the moment your career touched the lives of others. Impact and influence get created in those moments. And if you are doing even half the steps and tactics we laid out in this book, you have and are likely making a bigger impact on others than you may even realize. Which brings us to the final "Prepare for Impact" questions:

- Who did you impact today?
- How will you be remembered by the people you work with today?

Those are Ryan's true north leadership questions and ultimately the most important ones to ask about your leadership career.

Every day as a leader you have a chance to unleash what's inside your people—and *yourself*. We're *all* connected to something larger than ourselves. Everything you need to accomplish, all you desire in your business, and all you deserve in your life is inside you. It was put there for you. Our challenge and opportunity as leaders are to unleash more of what's inside our people *and* us and put that into the world on a consistent basis.

What a noble, *human* thing to do. What a beautiful thing to see the impact you have on people who then go out and become more than they thought they were capable of being. The opportunity to lead is a gift you've been given. Receive it—and steward it responsibly—with gratitude.

BEYOND THE 9 TACTICS

A MATTER OF TIME

RYAN KEEPS TWO DOCUMENTS permanently on his desktop. One is the eulogy for our father that we delivered together in 2011 after he died from cancer. The other is the result of a 2015 medical test when Ryan thought *he* had cancer:

IMPRESSION: Enhancing 2.8 x 2.1 x 4.8 cm mass within the anterior musculature of the distal left arm. Given speckled low signal density within the lesion, it is possible that this could represent a hemangioma. However, soft tissue sarcoma is thought more likely. The regions of low signal intensity within the mass may represent fibrous tissue as the lesion appears to arise along the intramuscular tendon.

It was early November when it all went down. It had been the biggest year of growth in Ryan's business—more than ninety events across the country—and his most challenging personally. Friendships and relationships are difficult to maintain when you spend hundreds of days on the road. Ryan was exhausted, and soon after he was in pain. It had started in his left forearm that summer. He thought he had hurt himself working out, but after a few months it still hurt. He couldn't fully straighten his arm. Before flying out for another event, he went to see his doctor. She didn't like what she saw and felt and told him to get an MRI that evening.

Ryan was on the plane the next day waiting to take off when the doctor called. He got off the plane.

"We got the results back, and it doesn't look good," she said. "There's a mass on your left bicep. We think it's sarcoma, and you need to see a specialist."

Ryan jumped right over shock, denial, pain, and guilt—the first stages of grief—and went straight to anger . . . with himself.

"Look what you did to yourself. You fucking idiot. *You* made this inside you. You know cancer runs in the family. You aren't taking care of yourself. *You* let this happen." Then came the tears. "I'm going to die like my dad."

Ryan called Chad, who knew something was wrong the moment Ryan started explaining what had happened.

"Oh my God."

"I'm not going to do the speech. I'm just going home and start dealing with this."

"Okay, call me when you get home. And call Mom."

It was almost two weeks before Ryan could get an appointment with a doctor who specialized in intramuscular tumors to determine the course of treatment. Plenty of time to add worry to his mix of emotions.

"He was in a low, man," Chad recalls. "He went right to the worst possible scenario: That he was going to be dead in two weeks. 'It's over. I'm going down.' All because they told him it looks like cancer. I knew I had to be at that appointment and told him I would."

"I was really emotional when he said that," Ryan says. "I felt completely alone. I was even more exhausted, if that was possible. I couldn't work. Things were falling apart. I was scared. The uncertainty was killing me. I had night sweats. I broke out in hives."

When Chad arrived, Ryan was a mess. He took one look at Ryan and launched into a pep talk. "We're going to get through this. We're going to meet with this doctor. If we don't think this doctor is right, we have other options."

Never once did Chad say *you*, and Ryan noticed. "He owned my problem with me. He wasn't going to let me think this was where our story ends. He shifted my mindset that night. Immediately I felt like I wasn't alone. I told him I could beat this."

That's when Chad pulled out the brochures. "And when we beat this, we are going to buy these Hublot watches. We are going to celebrate our victory."

Hublot is a Cowboys sponsor, and Ryan had seen some of their pieces when he visited. Chad knew he liked them. But Hublot watches are not inexpensive. Buying them would be a significant punctuation to the celebration.

We're buying watches? Ryan thought. Then he saw them for what they were: the pot of gold at the end of the rainbow. "In."

We headed out for a terrible dinner.

"We going to get a bottle of red?" Chad asked as the menus arrived.

"No, man. I don't drink alcohol anymore."

"What do you mean?"

"I'm fighting cancer."

* * *

Things went from the sublime to the ridiculous at the appointment the next day. The doctor said the tumor was near some nerve endings and shouldn't be biopsied, so he was going to go straight to surgery.

"Tell me about the surgery. What's the recovery period? Because I'm an athlete."

"What did you say?" Chad said before the doctor could respond.

"I'm an athlete."

"*Athlete*? What are you talking about? Dude, you're *not* an athlete."

The doctor looked at Chad, wondering where he came from.

"Yeah, I am."

"What kind of athlete are you?"

"I play basketball. I work out."

"That's not an athlete."

"Well, maybe I'm not an athlete, but I'm a performance artist."

"What?"

"I perform onstage."

Chad shook his head, and the doctor laughed. We went back and forth like that right through the debate about what the course of action should be and where the surgery should be performed.

Chad realized he couldn't be there for the surgery, but our mom could be, and that was enough.

In the days leading up to the surgery, Ryan thought about the eulogy we wrote for our father. The pastor had recommended that we not talk. That it was too emotional a time. We agreed to remember him together. We sat in a Starbucks for eight hours and wrote it all out, Chad constantly worrying that Ryan was going to "go keynote" as we spoke. We laughed at that and so much more. We argued a few times. We got emotional. And we ended up with that pretty cool eulogy that Ryan has saved on his desktop. Ryan was more determined than ever not to add his eulogy to Chad's desktop.

* * *

"Mom, do I have cancer?" Ryan whispered through the effects of the anesthesia wearing off.

"No. You are going to be okay!" she said, hugging him.

It was a benign tumor. It was over.

Ryan called Chad. "It's over, dude. Time to get the watches."

"Dude, you didn't have cancer."

"Yeah, but we got through it."

"You want me to drop fifteen grand on a watch for a benign tumor? Are you serious?"

We got the watches.

As we should have. Because when a doctor tells you that you have cancer or might have cancer—even when you don't—there's an inevitable moment of reflection and perspective shift. You ask yourself: *Where do I go from here?*

If anything has changed, it's with us personally in answering that question: Where do we go from here? We are thinking constantly about the time we have left—what Chad calls the "final third" of our lives—and what we want from it. We are thankful for the sacrifices we made early in our careers that allow us to do so many of the things we want to do now as we enter our final third. For us, that will still involve work, but it will be on our terms and centered around health, community, spirituality, nature, and love—building a life that is healthy both physically and mentally, spending more time outside, and being present in our most important relationships.

Thinking about the time you have left, how you spend it, and who you spend it with is critical, even without the darkness Ryan experienced. Which is why we didn't just get the watches. Ryan flew into Dallas to pick them out, and we had a big dinner together. As we opened them up, we gave speeches to each other. We raised a glass to our futures. We marked the moment and celebrated our love for each other—our brotherhood. We are in this together in the time we have left. Even if that means going to hell and back.

* * *

Why are you running this race, and who are you running it for?

That's the question Jesse asked us the night before the race in September 2022. To be clear, Jesse is Jesse Itzler, who is, among other things, the cofounder of Marquis Jet, an owner of the Atlanta Hawks, and a fantastic author and keynote speaker. He was asking us *and* 230 others this question the evening before Hell on the Hill—the hilliest half-marathon (13.1 miles) in the world, which his company, All Day Running Co., hosted in beautiful-middle-of-nowhere South Berwick, Maine.

We had been following Jesse since we read his book *Living With a SEAL: 31 Days Training with the Toughest Man on the Planet,* and Chad had become friendly with him after bringing him in to speak to the Cowboys' employees. When Chad made his list of fifty things he wanted to do before he died—fifty for his final third—he put Hell on the Hill on his list. When he asked Ryan to make it the Annual for 2022, Ryan was in. But we both agreed on one condition: This time, unspoken or not, this would not be a competition. This was about finishing—*together.*

When we first arrived and looked at the hill, it didn't look as bad as we made it out to be. And it's not. What makes Hell on the Hill grueling isn't the height of the hill but the cumulative elevation: Participants run sixty-five laps up and down it to equal 13.1 miles. To finish the race, you needed to complete those laps in four hours or less. That meant we needed to average under four minutes a lap to finish. This was going to be hard, but we knew it would be.

Jesse is all about doing hard things in community. "You only have so much time left," he said, "so how are you squeezing everything out of it for yourself and with others to make memories and remarkable shared experiences?" Jesse posed this question following dinner the night before the race. "Tomorrow will test you," he said, "but we should be grateful because so many people can't or aren't here anymore to do this."

That's when Jesse shared that exactly one hour into the race tomorrow at 8:00 a.m. the entire grounds would go silent for twenty minutes. No music. No loudspeakers. No talking. We would keep running, he explained, but he invited us during that silence to think about an answer to that very personal question: *Why are you running this race, and who are you running it for?*

The point of the question was to make us think about something larger ourselves. When the race gets hard, he explained, that purpose and thought of others can make you capable of so much more than if you were doing it just for yourself—more than you ever thought possible. Jesse shared he was running for and would be remembering his father, who he recently lost to Alzheimer's. He invited us to think about our answer that night and let us know that before we attacked the hill tomorrow he would invite a few people to share their answers with everyone.

At 5:00 a.m. the next day, we headed back to the grounds from the hotel, and over breakfast the shares started. It was a sea of emotion as people spoke vulnerably about trauma, tragedy, those they love, those they lost, and what really mattered the most. Hearing stories of others who had endured so much gave us an immense perspective and appreciation for each other and the lives we had. As they spoke, Ryan turned to Chad.

"Hey, man, why are you running? Who are you going to think about?"

Chad looked at Ryan. "I'm running for you. This is brotherhood, man. That's why I'm here. We're running together. That's what this is all about."

That's what this is all about. Brotherhood. Being together. Running for each other.

The words filled Ryan's heart as everyone headed to the top of the hill for the national anthem and the start of the race. Now we just needed to finish, and we didn't really have a plan of attack for that.

As the race started, we realized most everyone was taking the same approach: Walking up the hill and running down it. We followed their lead. But the amount of running was deceptive because you don't run down the same side of the hill you walk up. You run down the steep, far side of the hill to a flat path that curls around the bottom of the hill where you started. This was far more running than either of us expected, and we realized we probably had undertrained a bit. If we were just doing these laps for a workout, maybe we'd do fifteen of them. We needed more than four times that amount today.

Our recognition of the work in front of us was punctuated by some world-class athletes who lapped us on their way to running the whole thing in a little over two hours. Super cool to watch, but a constant reminder that we needed to keep less than half their pace to finish. And that's what we were doing. Halfway through, we got into a groove and were feeling optimistic.

Then, at lap fifty, Chad felt like his hamstrings were starting to cramp, and if he took another step he was going down.

"You might have to go. I may be out if I go into full leg cramps," Chad said. He told Ryan to go on as things got worse. "This cramp is so bad. I'm out."

"Nah," Ryan said. "If you're out, I'm out. We're finishing this together, so let's get some electrolytes, get a banana, chill for a minute, stretch and try to work it out, and see if you can go." He stood by Chad, waiting to see if his cramps would pass. They did, and we knew the wait had not cost us the finish line. If we continued the pace we had been on, we could finish the last fifteen laps with a little time to spare.

Then, with seven laps to go, Ryan looked at Chad and said, "I'm dizzy, and my body's breaking down."

Chad would have laughed if Ryan didn't look as awful as he sounded. While seven laps seemed like so little to go, it seemed physically impossible to Ryan at that moment. *I'm either dying right now or just physically can't do it,* he thought as he looked at the ambulances parked on the side of the hill for people in his condition.

But Chad wasn't about to let Ryan quit, just like Ryan didn't let him eight laps earlier. Chad wasn't going to go on without him. He started pumping up Ryan. "Come on, man, there are just seven laps left. You have got to find a way."

Ryan did. In that moment, he took Chad's words in and found a way to do more than he thought he was capable of. We finished with about three minutes to spare. If there had been one lap left, we wouldn't have made it.

Over dinner that night, we both acknowledged that if we had been by ourselves, we wouldn't have finished. We would have "died" on the hill. It took everything out of us, but by pulling each other along and through, we had made it. Together.

We will talk for the rest of our years about Hell on the Hill. How because of all the investment and effort we had put into our careers we were able to fly to Maine and do a half-marathon in the middle of the week to test the limits of our endurance and answer the call of brotherhood. The same brotherhood called us together for this book. We didn't have to write it—we *wanted* to. Too many people ignore that call to put themselves out there or wait until they think they have figured it all out to answer it. We haven't figured it out yet. But we are going to enjoy the journey together as we do—and share our success with each other and those around us.

Because we know our journey is not a race. It's a matter of time. What are you going to do with yours?

Ryan (left) and Chad crossing the finish line together at Hell on the Hill.

ENDNOTES

THE FOLLOWING SOURCES AND LINKS correspond to the research cited in the 30 Steps and 9 Tactics chapters.

Chapter 3
The 30 Steps to Success

2. PREPARATION

1 Biznology, "27 Surprising Facts About Salespeople Who Are Social Selling" (https://bit.ly/3Bhyvub).

2 Gartner, "The Future of Sales - Transformational Strategies for B2B Sales Organizations," as cited by many, including *Forbes* (https://bit.ly/3VwhhBv).

3. EDUCATION

3 Korn Ferry, "The Organisational X-Factor: Learning Agility" (https://bit.ly/3Y2PKcq).

4. TRAINING

4 The Brevet Group, "21 Mind-Blowing Sales Stats" (https://bit.ly/3VWbLYO).

7. KNOWLEDGE

5   LinkedIn, "State of Sales" 2021 (https://bit.ly/3VGkcrt).

9. SELL THE BENEFITS

6   Chip Heath & Dan Heath in *Made to Stick: Why Some Ideas Survive and Others Die*, as cited by many, including Adam Grant (https://bit.ly/3VCDyxG).

10. TIME MANAGEMENT

7   Acuity Training, "Time Management Statistics & Facts (New 2002 Research)" (https://bit.ly/3ixRWZd).

11. ASK FOR THE ORDER

8   Impact Business Partners, "90% of customers won't buy unless you ask" (https://bit.ly/3BgMyAi).

14. FOLLOW-UP

9   The Brevet Group, "21 Mind-Blowing Sales Stats" (https://bit.ly/3VWbLYO).

15. CORRESPONDENCE

10   *Small Business Trends*, "5 Reasons You Should Send Clients Handwritten Notes" (https://bit.ly/3UG9U9c).

16. CUSTOMER SERVICE

11   Salesforce, "The 6th State of Marketing Report Uncovers Trends to Navigate Change" (https://bit.ly/3Y7I7S0).

12   PricewaterhouseCoopers (PwC), "Experience is everything: Here's how to get it right" (https://bit.ly/3BhknRA).

13   Salesforce, "State of the Connected Customer" (https://bit.ly/3Y5nVAb).

17. KNOW YOUR COMPETITION

14   LinkedIn, "State of Sales," 2021 (https://bit.ly/3VGkcrt).

18. KNOW YOUR CLIENTS

15   The Brevet Group, "21 Mind-Blowing Sales Stats" (https://bit.ly/3VWbLYO).

22. RELATIONSHIPS

16   LinkedIn, "State of Sales," 2021 (https://bit.ly/3VGkcrt).

24. TEAMWORK

17 Zippia, "35+ Compelling Workplace Collaboration Statistics [2022]: The Importance of Teamwork" (https://bit.ly/3VFNpCQ).

26. MENTORING

18 Moving Ahead, "New UK research: Mentoring is improving gender balance in organisations" (https://bit.ly/3W0dnkk).

30. EXERCISE

19 Vagaro, "Vagaro Survey Finds Three-Quarters of Americans Believe Self-Care Activities Provide Stress Relief" (https://bit.ly/3HeWA8Z).

20 American Psychological Association, 2022, "Stress in America™" (https://bit.ly/3Hi48aQ).

Chapter 6
9 Tactics for Being a More Human-Centered Leader

OPENING

21 Gartner, as quoted in *Harvard Business Review*, "What Does It Mean to Be a Manager Today" (https://bit.ly/3PaiCvs).

22 Randstad, as cited in *Business Insider*, "Almost half of Gen Z and millennials would rather be unemployed than unhappy in a job, new research shows" (https://bit.ly/3HzX75F).

1. FOCUS ON THEIR DEVELOPMENT

23 Leadership IQ "The State of Leadership Development," 2020 (https://bit.ly/3F8HcbC).

2. GO FOR COFFEE

24 Dale Carnegie, "Get to Know Your Employees on a Personal Level" (https://bit.ly/3h1Me1D).

3. PRACTICE TRANSPARENCY

25 Davis Associates, "5 Reasons Why 57% of Employees Don't Trust Their Leaders" (https://bit.ly/3VEU2oY).

26 Fast Company, "The most confusing parts of job applications, according to graduating college students" (https://bit.ly/3HfSddN).

4. CREATE SAFETY

27   *Harvard Business Review*, "The Reason Your Team Won't Take Risks" (https://bit.ly/3P5Jz3r).

28   Gallup, "Is Quiet Quitting Real?" (https://bit.ly/3Paaz1R).

5. BUILD A TEAM ENVIRONMENT

29   *Journal of Experimental Social Psychology*, "Cues of working together fuel intrinsic motivation" (https://bit.ly/3XZtoZD).

6. CREATE CONNECTION—HAVE FUN!

30   Gartner, "Gartner Says HR Leaders Are Struggling to Adapt Current Organizational Culture to Support a Hybrid Workforce" (https://bit.ly/3FByyUh).

31   McKinsey, "Help your employees find purpose—or watch them leave" (https://bit.ly/3PtYgO5).

32   PricewaterhouseCoopers (PwC), "Putting Purpose to Work: A study of purpose in the workplace" (https://bit.ly/3iNZ6Zx).

33   Gallup, "The Increasing Importance of a Best Friend at Work" (https://bit.ly/3hjXGpb).

7. BE VULNERABLE

34   Leadership IQ, "The State of Leadership Development," 2020 (https://bit.ly/3F8HcbC).

35   PLOS ONE, "Oxytocin Increases the Influence of Public Service Advertisements" (https://bit.ly/3uxYhXC).

8. HAVE TOUGH CONVERSATIONS

36   LeadYouFirst.com, "Leaders Must Be Willing to Have Difficult Conversations" (https://bit.ly/3h5P0mi).

37   Harris Poll commissioned by Interact Studio, "Why Leaders Struggle to Give Employees Helpful Feedback" (https://bit.ly/3VEUuUd).

9. BE DECISIVE

38   SHRM, "How Leaders Can Make Better Decisions" (https://bit.ly/3W2sARV).

ACKNOWLEDGMENTS

From Ryan

I want to thank my coauthor and brother, Chad. He is my best friend and hands down one of the best, most human-centered leaders I know. I am forever grateful you took the ideas in that letter and used them in a way that had so much impact for others. I also know our best stories and shared experiences are still ahead of us.

Thank you, Jim Eber, for joining us on this journey and capturing the essence of the ideas and our relationship in such a special way.

Thank you, Naren Aryal, Myles Schrag, and the entire team at Amplify Publishing for your commitment to the project and persistence in bringing it to life.

A special thank you to my business manager, Lynn Mandinec. We've been together for most of this journey and your trust, confidence, and unwavering commitment has fueled our practice and made this book possible. I am forever grateful for your friendship and making the work so much fun.

Opportunity and mentorship matter. I owe an incredible debt of gratitude to Tom Richey and especially to John Stepien for teaching me so much about leadership. Those lessons are only superseded by what you taught me about life and living well. Thank you.

I want to thank Scot Cohen. Your unwavering confidence and commitment to our friendship have been instrumental to my growth and fulfillment. I am so lucky to have such a dear friend. I want to thank my family: Mom and Dad. Brooke. Greg and Tracey. Ben, Allie, Ella, Evan, and Jayce. My life is enriched because I am a part of yours.

I am so grateful for Seth Mattison, Josh Linkner, and Peter Sheahan. Working together has been the most rewarding professional experience of my life. Thank you for your friendship. Life is better together and I look forward to sharing so much joy and impact together on the journey forward.

I want to thank the ImpactEleven team and community. I am so proud of what we are creating and truly believe we are better together.

There is no place like home. A special, heartfelt thank you to my community in Minneapolis and the bonds of friendship that will endure through this lifetime. Life is meant to be lived this way.

I want to thank all the people who put the 30 Steps into practice. Thank you for seeing something in those words and ideas that compelled you to answer the call. I never imagined they would be used this way, but I am grateful they offered some value and we got to capture the origin story here.

From Chad

I want to start by thanking my coauthor and brother, Ryan. You have been my mentor, best friend, and trusted advisor. Without your guidance, many of the experiences written in this book would not have been possible. I'm especially grateful for your development of the 30 Steps and receiving those in the mail twenty-nine years ago.

Thank you to Jim Eber for helping us put this book together. You have an amazing talent, and I am so appreciative of how you captured our thoughts on these pages. In addition, I made a new friend and have found a way to overlook your affinity for another NFL team in the same division.

I also want to thank my family: my wife, Tracey, and my kids, Ben and Allie. Tracey, thank you for your incredible support of my career all these years. It means everything to me. Ben and Allie, you inspire me always to do my best and lead by example. I love you all so much.

Early in my career, I had a group of people take me under their wings. They mentored me, taught me, challenged me, and set me up for success. I'm so appreciative of the opportunity I had to learn from John Ciszewski, Tom Wilson, Jim Kahler, Buffy Filippell, and Michael Yormark.

Working for the Dallas Cowboys has been beyond rewarding, both personally and professionally. I want to thank the Jones family—Jerry, Gene, Stephen, Charlotte, and Jerry Jr.—for treating me like family and providing me with more opportunities than I knew existed.

And to my friends at Legends. What a special ride we are on. To be a part of something that started from scratch and to see where we are today has been so rewarding. The best part of all is to do it with this special team. Thank you, Shervin Mirhashemi, Dan Smith, Bill Rhoda, John Ruzich, Mike Tomon, and Chris Hibbs.

Last, I have been fortunate through my career to have some of the most talented and loyal people join me for the long ride. They have also become my best friends in life. Thank you, Mike Ondrejko, Doug Dawson, Eric Sudol, Delanie Foley, and Todd Fleming. How lucky am I to be on this journey with all of you. I love and appreciate you so much.

ABOUT THE AUTHORS

RYAN ESTIS is a globally recognized sales and leadership expert, keynote speaker, and co-founder of ImpactEleven, a hyper-growth startup community of thought leaders. A former Fortune 500 Chief Revenue Officer, Ryan has spent his career in the trenches, leading high-performance teams, and building a client roster of category-leading brands.

CHAD ESTIS serves as the Executive Vice President of Business Operations for the Dallas Cowboys and AT&T Stadium and Executive Vice President for Legends, a global premium experiences company that specializes in delivering holistic solutions for sports and entertainment organizations and venues. Though he's had much success growing teams' bottom lines, the largest impact of Chad's career has been on his people.